Larceny in the Aisles

JOE,

CONGRATULATIONS ON
RETIREMENT! I WOULD
BET YOU COULD HAVE
CONTRIBUTED TO THIS BOOK.

ENJOY

Larceny in the Aisles

Stories from a Supermarket Manager

By Mark Scamman
Illustrated by Destinee Almeida

978-0-578-36157-4

Cover and inside illustrations by Destinee Almeida
Copy editing and book design by Janice Beetle Books, LLC

Dedication

To Amy, Robby, and Kelsey.

Contents

Illustrations

Foreword

When I was a teenager, I had several friends who routinely shoplifted from a large department store in the local mall. Their habit began small, with things like Chapstick and rouge they could tuck in a pocket, escalating to entire outfits, shoes, and other items their parents couldn't afford.

They would go in a store dressing room, remove their own clothes, put on clothes they had yet to purchase, layer their own outfit on top, and then leave—just like that. They had other techniques for items they couldn't wear home.

I heard these stories after the crimes were committed and always felt a wave of relief that I hadn't been with them. Early on, though, I was part of a spree that involved snitching a lip gloss. I was terrified because I clearly knew right from wrong, but I did not listen to that little voice in my head that said, "Don't do it."

I wanted those girls to like me. I wanted to fit in.

I did it, even though I had heard stories of other teenaged girls getting caught and hauled up into the store's office, where a manager would call either their parents, or the police, or both.

Peer pressure is a powerful thing. But when my friends upped their stakes, I stopped going to the mall with them. I listened to that little voice, finally. I didn't want to be involved, partly because I feared the consequences and partly because I could envision the sad face my father would wear when he picked me up at the store office. He would have been shamed and disappointed, and I couldn't do that to him.

In reading Mark's book, Larceny in the Aisles, I could relate to the stories about teenagers stealing from the grocery store, like the young girls in Chapter 32. They reminded me of my few unpleasant excursions, although I would never have been fresh to a store manager if apprehended; I would have dissolved in tears.

The broad range of tales that Mark tells, about shoplifters of all ages and backgrounds, astounds me. This book gives one a window into theft that you might not imagine.

Readers see an extensive range of things that people steal, as well a list equally long of the varying motivations.

Seniors stealing because they need an ingredient they can't afford for a special holiday meal.

People with alcohol dependency stealing extract or medication because it contains alcohol.

Women stealing pregnancy kits—and using them in the store's bathroom.

Organized crime rings stealing everything from baby formula to manufacture drugs to high-end meats they will sell to convenience store owners to make money to buy drugs.

Mothers teaching their kids to steal, sometimes just for the "fun" of it.

Mark's stories, gathered over a full career as a manager in a supermarket chain, entertained me and also enlightened me.

Mark tells readers about the laws that protect retailers from crime and what the process looks like after a criminal is apprehended and charged. More disturbing, though, he shows us that the laws are changing, state to state, and protections for retailers are being diminished so that store owners aren't always able to recoup what they've lost.

Reading Larceny in the Aisles is sure to engage you, and it may also make you pay more attention to the laws that protect retailers. Perhaps it might inspire you to better understand the laws in your state and to advocate on behalf of retailers if you think they don't go far enough.

Consequences to crime are of the utmost importance—whether we are talking about homicide or shoplifting. Those who consider committing an illegal act should know they are taking a grave risk.

Because not everyone has a conscience—or a father they wish to protect.

Janice Beetle

Introduction: Shoplifting

Shopping at the supermarket might never be the same for you after reading these fifty unique shoplifting stories. They'll have you wondering if the customer in the aisle with you is a thief.

As a young grocery store manager back in the early nineties, I was involved with a variety of shoplifting incidents, approximately two hundred and fifty in my first five years in management. The whole idea of stealing from a grocery store really struck a nerve with me. It soon became apparent that shoplifting was a common occurrence not limited to gender, age, race, or social standing.

I had witnessed shoplifting when I was coming up through the ranks, but not to the degree I saw when I began looking for shoplifters in earnest.

The first store location I managed was in a vacation area bordered by a small college in New England. You might not think it was a shoplifting mecca, but it was. A third of the people caught were college students. Another third were senior citizens. The other third were common thieves or people down on their luck.

Over the years, I told friends and family members shoplifting stories. Some made them laugh, some made them cry, and some just made them angry. I started to document the tales, thinking someday I would compile them in a book.

For Christmas 2020, I got a Chromebook laptop—much better than pencil and paper. I started to put words to all the stories about shoplifters I had documented in my forty-plus-year career as a supermarket store manager. Shoplifting was one key part of managing a store. You had to protect the bottom line.

During my career, I caught nearly one thousand shoplifters. I worked in thirteen stores that covered two states. These are my stories. Imagine all the other stories that managers, and loss-prevention personnel in supermarkets, clothing stores, big-box stores, home-improvement stores, etc. could tell. Each must have hundreds. That is an awful lot of shoplifting going on in this country today. Estimated losses for shoplifting annually are in the billions of dollars. The products stolen range from a pack of gum to a carriage full of groceries.

Before I got the idea to write this book, when I tried to find books on shoplifting, it was difficult. Most were about how to prevent shoplifting, or the economic results of the act of shoplifting. I also found books about kleptomania. This book about shoplifting is different. I wanted to tell the stories of individual incidents that I have dealt with over all my years as a store manager.

Many of the incidents I experienced are similar, but each is unique and has its own character. There are so many ways to shoplift, different ways the shoplifter gets caught—enough to write a couple of books.

The stories in this book are all from actual incidents. All the shoplifters were caught by me or by my staff in a team effort. Several of them were reported by customers and employees as well. The shoplifters are nameless. All arrests are public record. The police and towns are real, but anonymous.

Shoplifters are not limited to a specific color or race. Various age groups are portrayed in the book only to show the diversity. I portray each offender's gender accurately. According to my sample of nearly one thousand shoplifters, the females shoplifted over sixty percent of the time as compared to the men.

Along with the stories of actual shoplifting incidents is information offered to educate the reader about shoplifting and some of the nuances and provisions of the law. I look at civil recovery, grand larceny, willful concealment, kleptomania, organized crime rings, police involvement, communication, and what it's like in the courtroom with a judge.

That there are senior citizens who can't afford to eat, who steal because they are hungry, should be a wake-up call of grave concern to us all. Over four hundred shoplifting incidents involved senior citizens, and over one hundred got away. These older adults are just trying to survive. Sometimes, they just want that little extra something that we take for granted. The social security system that was put in place to care for our friends, neighbors, and loved ones in their golden years has obviously failed.

Opioid-addicted shoplifters also account for hundreds of incidents; they were easy to spot but not so easy to contain or arrest. If a shoplifter was high, he or she was usually very cooperative, docile, easy to control, and I had each one arrested. It's the only way I thought they could get help—by getting entered in the system and standing before a judge. If a person needed a fix and was stealing to support his next score, that person was not thinking straight. When confronted, the shoplifter often tried to run, and often, the incident ended in a struggle. That shoplifter was arrested.

Shoplifters who stole while shopping with their kids were especially troubling to me. There were easily over a hundred incidents that I documented. Kids are sponges and learn from their parents. The older the kids were, the more they saw. There were many kids who were in on the shoplifting—directed by the adults in the strategy of it, what to do. These kids will steal when they grow up, no doubt.

My dealings with parents of minors who were caught shoplifting elicited a variety of responses; some thanked me, others nearly accused me of being at fault. Sometimes, when I called a parent and not the police, I wished I had called the police. This was very rare; most parents were very thankful that I called them. But a parent is a parent, and when it comes to their children, I was apt to get the kind of response you'd get from mama bear protecting her cub.

I called one parent early in my career and told her that her fourteen-year-old daughter had been caught shoplifting from the store. The mother thought I was her boyfriend, pranking her, because he had just dropped the girl off.

I would like to thank all my family and friends. My co-workers, managers, and supervisors I worked for were instrumental in helping me learn about shoplifting and teaching me the laws around it, so we could all catch as many shoplifters as we did. The store managers who came up through the ranks, as I did, have their own stories to tell. Some have more stories; some less. Some managers shared their stories with me, and those appear in a later chapter of the book. I also am grateful to the many customers who lent a hand when we were trying to control a shoplifter—for their help in a crisis and for being loyal.

To the many police departments and officers I have dealt with over the years, I would like to say: Your job is not getting any easier, and I personally applaud all your efforts. There was never a bad incident in the many arrests that we made together. Defunding your departments will not help with the shoplifting problem, and most likely will push the crime further down the food chain, turning into a free-for-all. Thank you for your service.

Chapter 1
Shoplifting 101

Wikipedia defines shoplifting as "the theft of goods from an open retail establishment, typically by concealing a store item on one's person, in pockets, under clothes, or in a bag, and leaving the store without paying."

Shoplifting is not front-page news. It is not something you'd expect to see explicit posts about on your Twitter feed—or any social media feed, for that matter. Shoplifting is buried in the depths of news articles.

If you looked for stories about shoplifting, though, you could definitely find some. You might be apt to learn that a shoplifting conviction in the late 1800s would result in a prison term of five years in jail. The shoplifter would go to prison for the full five years.

Today, a shoplifting conviction carries a slap on the wrist and possibly a one-hundred-dollar fine, and probation.

Shoplifting is a broad term that covers a lot of offenses.

There are more ways to be charged for shoplifting than just concealing an item and walking out the door without paying for that item. If you alter or change a price of a product to lower its value and defraud the store in that way, it is considered shoplifting.

If you knowingly bring back stolen items to the store to exchange for cash or a gift card, it is considered shoplifting.

You also cannot possess a theft-detection-shielding device or coated bag to conceal merchandise from an electronic theft detector. That is considered shoplifting. Walking out of a store with a carriage full of merchandise, not paid for, is considered shoplifting. If you eat your way around a store and do not pay for what you consume, you are shoplifting.

Once a shoplifter is caught, the value of the pilfered product, or products, determines the level of charges brought against the shoplifter. Shoplifting crimes vary from state to state, and the consequences vary as well.

Only a few states, one being New Hampshire, allow for a merchant to apprehend a suspect after an item is concealed—before they leave the store. If a shopper puts an item in his or her pocket, purse, or baby stroller, and it is concealed, by law in New Hampshire, that act is willful concealment. You can be arrested before you leave the store, even if you do not go past the point of sale. This arrest usually results in a misdemeanor finding, a lesser charge than shoplifting.

With the popularity of reusable bags over the years, concealment became tough to call. A lot of customers shopped by filling their reusable bags, rather than using the store baskets. Most police departments now, even in New Hampshire, want the shoplifter to get past the point of sale—the registers—before they will make an arrest. This way there is no doubt that the shopper's intention was to steal. For this reason, I wouldn't be surprised if willful concealment charges faded away.

In one small county of eastern Massachusetts, there was recently an emerging agenda to make it easier for criminals to get away with crime. Racheal Rollins was elected Suffolk County District Attorney in the state of Massachusetts in 2018. Her platform was to decriminalize a number of non-violent crimes, including drug possession with intent to distribute, larceny under two hundred and fifty dollars, and shoplifting.

I object, in particular, to her stance on shoplifting, given my experience. What is a merchant to do if shoplifting isn't a crime when someone steals from them? How about the people the crime hurts? The merchant and shop owners? The consumers, who ultimately pay for the loss of revenue?

Ms. Rollins' platform of reform acknowledges that there is plenty to change, but allowing people to steal with little or no consequences for their actions is not an answer. Can you imagine what would happen if there were no criminal charges for shoplifting? There would literally be a free-for-all. Looting could take on a whole new meaning.

In a May 16, 2019, article in the *Boston Herald*, Sean Philip Cotter offered a piece on what could happen if Rachael Rollins' no-prosecute agenda found footing.

Cotter's piece focused on Glenn Kerivan, who watched a news report of Rollins' no-prosecute list on TV while he was in prison. Shortly after his release, Kerivan couldn't believe it when he got busted in Weymouth, Massachusetts, for shoplifting $126 worth of groceries from Stop & Shop. He thought Ms. Rollins' idea had come to fruition, and it was no longer a crime to shoplift. He thought the cops who arrested him were making a mistake. He believed Suffolk County District Attorney Rollins no longer prosecuted shoplifting charges.

Kerivan was arrested on May 9, 2019. He pleaded guilty the following day and was charged a five-hundred-dollar fine. The problem for Kerivan was he was not in Suffolk County when he shoplifted. He was in Weymouth, which is in Norfolk County, where prosecutors take shoplifting seriously.

Michael O'Keefe, district attorney for the Cape and Islands, said in Cotter's *Herald* report, "...thieves thinking it's open season is a logical conclusion of a list like Rollins' ...I would like people to be assured that irrespective of what happens in Suffolk County, shoplifting is most certainly a crime in the rest of Massachusetts."

In the same article, Mayor Robert Hedlund of Weymouth said that Kerivan "should have studied his geography." He warned shoplifters that they would be arrested if caught shoplifting in his city.

Chapter 2
A Typical Shoplifting Incident

M ost shoplifting incidents I managed or was involved in were handled rather quickly and without much embarrassment to the individual who was implicated. Usually, an employee or member of management saw something suspicious and reported it. We then kept an eye on that individual.

There were a number of cameras in our building. Some were fixed, but a lot were moveable—left to right, up and down—and they also could zoom in and out. The cameras had high-quality lenses and could hone in on the date on a penny.

The cameras gave us a lot of information, and they didn't lie, but you still needed to follow the suspect until he or she passed the point of sale—the registers. You had to be sure a suspected shoplifter had in his or her possession the item you believed was concealed. You had to be one hundred percent certain.

On some occasions, I saw suspected shoplifters either feel they were being watched or otherwise get spooked. They would dump whatever they had in their possession in another aisle. If an employee didn't witness this unloading and continued to confront them, the store, or I—or both of us—could become liable. This is why it was important to have certainty before lodging an accusation.

An incident comes to mind from spring 2014 as representing most of the shoplifting cases I have been involved in over the years. One of my employees told me a female in the health and beauty aisle had put what the employee thought was an Olay beauty product in the customer's pocketbook.

We went to the camera room and watched our suspect. A few moments later, she put a large bottle of Advil in her purse. Now, I was not certain she was in possession of the Olay cream, because I didn't witness that theft, but I was sure about the Advil she put in her pocketbook. If there had been time, I could have rewound the camera feed to watch her take the Olay beauty product, but there wasn't. We did have enough evidence to confront her.

I watched the customer until she got to the registers. I also informed my front-end manager about what was happening. The customer took her wallet out of her purse before she got to the register, which we knew to be a sign that she would not open her purse at the register. She was probably fearful the product might be visible in her pocketbook.

Normally, if I was on watch, I would confront the shoplifter, as I did with this individual. On occasion, I would have another member of management with me to learn how to approach a suspected shoplifter. There were protocols to follow.

That moment just before a confrontation was always a butterflies-in-the-stomach time for me, whether the suspect was a child or a senior citizen. From my first shoplifter to my last, the feeling was always the same.

I learned from experience, though, which shoplifters would not pose a problem and which would become trouble. I did not feel that female would be difficult. When she was done checking out, I met her near the exit.

Because, by law, you cannot accuse someone of taking something even when you are one hundred percent certain, I asked, "Did you forget to pay for the Advil you have in your pocketbook?"

She hesitated, realized she was caught, and said, "Oh, I didn't realize I put it in there." She continued, "I would like to pay for it."

"Okay, let's go to my office so we can settle this," I said, and we went to the office.

When there is a female suspect, you must have a female witness. If you are a female manager and have a male suspect, you must have a male witness. Protocols also forbade one from taking a suspect to the office alone, one on one. Always, you had to have a witness present.

The female employee who'd reported that incident to me was waiting in the office to serve as the witness. The shoplifter took out the Advil and put it on my desk. We were all seated. I asked her about the Olay beauty product she had in her bag as well. She was a little shocked but reached in, took out the Olay, and placed it on my desk.

"Do you have anything else," I asked.

She said no and opened her pocketbook so I could see inside. I asked my female employee to look inside the pocketbook as well. She also didn't see anything else that looked like it belonged to our store.

I told the customer, "This is shoplifting." I told her what she had done was a crime and asked her if she thought I should call the police. She said, "no."

When the police are called, arrest is nearly a certainty. Our Olay shoplifter could have been taken in a police cruiser to the police station, and possibly, she would have been locked up in a holding cell. She would have been released with a court date to appear before a judge.

In court, she likely would have pled guilty, and fines would range between one and two hundred dollars, or more. She would have been put on probation, and her name would have made the local newspaper. If the incident was her first offense, it would have been recorded as such, and she would suddenly have a criminal record.

Now, I don't know if that shoplifter had a record, but I know she did not want the police to be involved.

I explained that the law provided her with an option to arrest; she could pay what was called a civil recovery fee, which was essentially a fine that provided restitution to the merchant for the cost of surveillance and time spent apprehending a shoplifter. This fee did not cover the cost of goods stolen; the shoplifter could pay for those separately. The benefit to the shoplifter was avoiding embarrassment, police involvement, and court appearances; they could put a stop to the incident in the moment.

Each state in the United States has its own guidelines for civil recovery, which must be followed judiciously and in an exacting manner. At the time of this incident, Massachusetts law provided not more than five hundred dollars in restitution, and New Hampshire law was not more than three hundred, for each shoplifting incident.

This customer agreed to pay the restitution. She filled out the appropriate paperwork and paid fifty dollars with a credit card. She also paid for the Olay and Advil separately, as the stolen product is not part of the restitution paid to the merchant. I explained to her that the charge against her would then be confidential; no one else would learn about it. "However," I told her, "If you are caught shoplifting again, I will have to call the police and have you arrested."

Before the customer left the office that day, I explained to her she could still shop at our store as long as she didn't steal from us again. "When you steal, it affects me and all of my employees," I told her.

She promised she wouldn't shoplift again, got her carriage of groceries, and left.

This was an easy incident to handle. Most of the remaining chapters in this book illustrate that confronting shoplifters was not as calm a process as in this case. Many shoplifters also did not show appreciation, even though I felt offering shoplifters I caught the option of civil recovery was giving them a break. I only presented this possibility if, and only if, the shoplifter was cooperative—to save the individual from embarrassment.

Once, I caught a female stealing forty dollars' worth of groceries. After she decided to go with the civil recovery law, she told me she could not pay her oil bill. I explained to her that we could call the police, and she could take her oil bill issue up with a judge. I also told her the judge would more than likely fine her. She reluctantly paid civil recovery.

On another occasion, in 1995, I caught a professor who taught at a prestigious New England private high school. He stole a pen. The professor was quite arrogant as I explained to him that he would be arrested by the police in this small town, even for stealing a pen. He finally agreed to the maximum civil recovery at the time, which was two hundred dollars in restitution. He said he had his reputation to protect.

Chapter 3
Baby Formula, Hypodermic Needle

I t was a cold Sunday night in the winter of 2011, and business was on the slow side. There had been a snowstorm the night before, and folks were still digging out. One hour to go, and I would be heading home.

While taking a last lap around the store, checking departments and gathering overstock merchandise that customers decided they did not want, I noticed a man with a long, black trench coat and skullcap entering the store. He did not take a carriage and went down the health and beauty aids (HBA) aisle, in which baby formula was stocked. I made my way to the camera room to see what he was up to. He was acting suspicious, looking around quite a bit. I kept the surveillance fixed on him.

After a minute or so, the man in the black trench coat began putting cans of powdered baby formula inside his coat. He must have had a secret pocket. I called the associate manager on his portable phone, and he met me at the office. I showed him what was happening. He covered one exit, and I watched the other. I had the office clerk call the police so they could get there quickly. This guy was going to be arrested, and I was pretty sure it would not go smoothly. The man with the black trench coat was going to be trouble and certainly would not want to go to our office peacefully.

Still, we had to follow protocols when confronting him: Don't accuse; just treat him as we would any other customer.

As the man in the black trench coat came my way, I stepped in front of him at the door. He passed by the registers without paying. I asked him if he forgot to pay for the number of baby formula cans he had in his coat. He looked at me and had the deer-in-the-headlights look. My associate manager then joined us to assist me. If the shoplifter had left the store, we would not have been allowed to pursue—again, a company policy we had to adhere to.

The police had been called, and if the shoplifter made it outside, it would be up to them to apprehend this guy.

In the moment of confrontation, one of three things typically happens:

Confession. As with the Olay offender in Chapter 2, shoplifters realize they've been caught. They put their heads down, droop their shoulders, and more often than not, say, "It was my first time," or "I would like to pay for the item." The Confessor is cooperative and comes to the office without incident. This was the case in seventy percent of the nearly one thousand shoplifting cases I was involved with in my career.

Wait and see. In another possible scenario, the shoplifter realizes he or she has been caught and is outnumbered. This type of offender wants to run but waits for an opening. The Wait and See shoplifter usually heads back into the store because management is focused on blocking the way outside.

Run. In the last scenario, the accused runs, trying to get away instantly. This is what the man in the black trench coat full of baby formula tried to do. He tried to get away.

There was a struggle. The police had not arrived yet.

My associate manager and I tried to keep the baby formula guy from leaving. We all ended up on the floor, and baby formula cans were rolling all over the place. It was a struggle to try to contain the suspect, and then, suddenly, there was a helping hand and a knee placed on the shoplifter's shoulder.

The assist came from a customer who was in line at the checkout, witnessing what was happening. This customer was a good-sized man, about two hundred and fifty pounds, and with his extra pair of hands, the shoplifter slowed, then stopped, his struggle.

While waiting for the police to arrive, a group of customers gathered to watch the situation unfold. Employees were picking up the loose baby formula cans on the floor, and there was more in the shoplifter's trench coat.

While I was lying on the ground, holding the shoplifter by the waist, two ladies watching in the group of onlookers cautiously approached me. They knew I was the store manager. One lady leaned down and asked if she could pay for the baby formula so the shoplifter could feed his child.

Nice gesture, but this guy was going to sell this formula for pennies on the dollar so he could fund his drug habit. I tried to explain, from my unenviable position on the floor, that formula was valuable to large-scale criminals in the manufacture of illegal drugs, such as cocaine and heroin; cans of powdered formula are mixed into those drugs to extend the supply.

"This guy isn't feeding his baby," I told the compassionate women. "He will sell the formula so he can buy drugs." They looked at me in shock, thinking I was lying. They'd probably never witnessed a shoplifting incident.

Two police officers finally showed up what felt like a half hour later, but really only three or four minutes had passed. While one officer cuffed the shoplifter, the other said, "Sharp."

I looked down, where the officer was looking, and there it was: a hypodermic needle. My feet were close to the syringe, but I didn't think much of it at the moment. My focus was on thanking the officers and the customer who came to our aid. Without that customer's help, the trench coat guy could easily have gotten away.

I also noticed the two ladies talking to an officer; they still wanted to pay to feed the shoplifter's baby. The officer was respectful, but you could also see a smirk on his face as he showed them the needle and also tried to explain the situation. I never saw those women again, but to this day, I imagine they still think that formula shoplifter was trying to feed an infant.

Finally, the situation on the sales floor was cleaned up, and police took the shoplifting suspect to the station to be booked. The officers gave me a case number, and I headed to the office to write a report. When I sat down, the adrenaline wore off, and I felt a pinch on top of my right foot. I took off my shoe and sock; right above the toe of the shoe was a red mark. I realized I'd been jabbed by the needle in the struggle.

My adrenaline high shifted to despair. Contracting HIV was all I could think about for the next hour. My associate manager was in the office with me and told me I should get the red wound evaluated by a doctor. I immediately left and decided to go to the emergency room closest to my home.

I arrived about six that Sunday night. There was a little bit of a wait, but I finally got in to see the doctor. He looked at the red mark as I told him the situation and explained what had just happened at the store. Here are the odds he recounted to me: If the needle hit the bone, my chance of contracting HIV might have been one in five million. If the needle hit muscle, the chance rose to one in three million.

I was offered medication the size of horse pills for thirty days, but the doctor said it would probably make me extremely sick. He indicated that treatment for HIV had come a long way and suggested I do nothing but wait it out.

A colleague in another store had recently been jabbed by a needle, and he took the medicine. The treatment indeed made him so sick he was barely able to work during those thirty days. I did not want to deal with that. I was a little unsettled for a couple of weeks, but nothing ever happened to me. After a couple of months, I went back for a blood test. It came back negative for HIV, and I was quite relieved. I am still fine today.

Chapter 4
More Baby Formula, The Sisters

This baby formula incident involves two sisters who had stolen from the supermarket on numerous occasions in 2014, but they were never caught. Multiple times we realized, after the fact, that they had gotten away.

These two sisters worked very quickly, in and out of the store in five minutes. Every time we realized they had stolen from us again, we called the police to report it. Each time the sisters came in, they took a few more cans of baby formula than they did the previous visit. They were becoming much bolder.

One day, they deviated from their normal routine.

The sisters typically stole at night, always around closing time. This time, they showed up at three o'clock in the afternoon on a Sunday. I don't remember how I knew they were in the store, but we were watching them. The girls had empty, very large shoulder bags. They had picked up a carriage and put their shoulder bags in the shopping cart's baby seat. Then they headed straight for the baby formula section.

They proceeded to put into their shopping cart twelve cans of powdered baby formula. I was pretty sure they were drug addicts and would sell this formula to get cash for their next fix. This particular baby formula was the best seller, and only one was allowed to be purchased with assistance provided by Women, Infants, and Children (WIC), a federal program that assists low-income woman, infants, and children under five years old. The program provides funding for nutritious foods and education on eating a healthy diet.

A convenience store, mom-and-pop establishment, or a bodega would pay the shoplifting sisters fifty percent of the value for the WIC-approved baby formula and then charge persons shopping in their stores the full retail price. That is a fifty percent markup. Far more than if the establishment bought the baby formula through proper channels. This is obviously against the law.

The sisters and their carriage of goods were in the front main aisle. They had filled their shoulder bags with what they had in the carriage. Not only did they have formula, but they'd stopped by the meat department and picked up some steaks as well. They did this next to a display in the front main aisle of the store. This was very much in the open, and the sisters really did not try to hide their thievery.

We were waiting for them. I was outside, and my associate manager alerted me they were leaving the building. They did not pay for what they had in their pocketbooks. I met them in the vestibule and asked them why they hadn't paid for the baby formula. They didn't give me any trouble, and we headed back inside, to my office.

The police had been called and provided the incident numbers from the multiple times the two had gotten away. When the officers arrived, they gave me an incident number for this case. Not much was said in the office. The sisters offered their identification information, and that was the first time I realized they were sisters. They did not look anything alike.

The officers handcuffed the female shoplifters, and out to the cruiser the sisters went. I don't recall what their punishment was, but we did get restitution from all previous incidents.

Chapter 5
Even More Baby Formula

This incident was especially frustrating to me as I was supervising a large order for a local town's year-end sports party when it happened. It was a Sunday in 2014, and I happened to be on the surveillance camera during my lunch break, watching the HBA aisle. I had left the surveillance office for about fifteen or twenty minutes to put together the spaghetti supper order for the soccer club.

After the order was complete, I went back to the security office to finish my sandwich. Back to watching the HBA aisle. I noticed the baby formula section was completely empty. It had been nearly full minutes earlier. We'd been hit.

I went to play back the video feed, and sure enough, a couple—a male and female—had wiped out the shelf. They put all the formula in one carriage and covered it with a large package of toilet tissue, then walked right out the door. This was well over five hundred dollars of goods; another pair of thieves had gotten away. Time was not on my side for this one. I called the police.

Officers came and looked at the video and knew who the shoplifters were. They did not know their names, but the pair of shoplifters had hit a number of stores in town that carried baby formula. The officer said they had not been caught yet. Same MO (modus operandi): load up the carriage with baby formula, cover it, and walk out the door. The male kept an eye out while the female shoplifter went right out the front door. Then the male quickly followed. The officer gave me an incident number and left.

The same officer who responded to this shoplifting event came back a couple weeks later to tell me this twosome had finally been caught. The store would probably not get restitution, though, as these shoplifters were indigent, and may have had a serious drug problem.

In 2016, it was estimated that stolen baby formula cost merchants over four billion dollars annually. That made it easy to decide to take it off the shelves and put it under lock and key.

Going forward, consumers had to ask for baby formula.

Chapter 6
The Jumper

One evening in 2012 before the end of my shift, I had about a half hour to fill and decided to do some surveillance via the cameras. That was like fishing, and there was plenty of bait between the health and beauty aids, laundry detergent, and vitamins and supplements.

After about fifteen minutes, I noticed a male, about 5'10", with an athletic build, wearing what appeared to be a new workout suit. He was nervously looking up and down the supplement aisle. He had two bottles of supplements, one in each hand. With one last look, he smoothly put the supplements in his pockets—one on the left and the other on the right. I did not know what the actual supplements were, only that he had taken them from the shelf.

Several managers were on duty, and I contacted the two closest to me on their portables to assist. We covered the exits and waited for the shoplifter to pass the registers. The individual came my way, and I stepped in front of him to block the entrance. I asked if he forgot to pay for the supplements he had in his pockets. To my relief he looked at me and dropped his shoulders. He offered to pay for them.

I said, "We can settle this in the office."

Once there, the shoplifter was given two choices: call the police or pay civil recovery. This guy did not want the police to be called and agreed to pay civil recovery. The shoplifter was cooperative to this point, and we moved forward with the civil recovery paperwork.

It was now well past five o'clock and time for me to go home. My assistant manager was more than capable of finishing up the paperwork.

I was at the bottom of the stairs when my assistant called to me to let me know the shoplifter did not have identification. Valid ID was required to complete the civil recovery form; I told my assistant to call the police, as the only other alternative at that point was to let the accused free.

Not even ten seconds later, I heard commotion and footsteps running down the stairs. I was at the door and heard from above that the shoplifter was trying to get away. I tried to block the door, but he managed to open it slightly. My managers were also coming down the stairs to apprehend our criminal. Just in time, another customer—the father of an employee—came to our aid and helped me keep the door closed.

During the uproar, one of the service center clerks called the police. The dispatcher kept the clerk on the line as the shoplifter was escorted back up to the office above the service center. Within thirty seconds, the shoplifter again tried to get away. This time he vaulted over the small wall in my office, dropping down onto the ledge above our service center. To escape, he would have had to jump about eight feet to the ground in front of the service center. He crept forward on the ledge and then jumped. I was still watching as he hit the ground and stumbled. A crowd of onlookers, customers, employees, and myself, were able to detain him, keeping him on the floor.

It had been a long day, and I had just realized I would be getting home late. It wasn't very often my emotions got the best of me, but this shoplifter brought them all out. While I had a knee on his shoulder, I let loose.

"Why are you stealing from me?" I screamed at him. I repeated the question a couple of times until the police arrived.

I suspect that guy might have had a record or a warrant out for his arrest, making escape seem to him like the only option.

Writing the report, we had to seek restitution from the district attorney. The shoplifter broke the door to the office and its door handle. He broke a display case when he jumped. Although it took several months, our store did receive a check from the local clerk of courts to cover the cost of repairs.

Chapter 7
Angel in the Catwalk

When I first became manager of my own store in 1989, there were no surveillance cameras. Shoplifters were observed from a second-story catwalk that ran the length of the back of the store. We accessed it from a set of rear stairs.

There were two-way mirrors set up about eye level on the catwalk. This allowed the store below to be watched by a person manning the catwalk. There were a half dozen phones placed on the wall underneath the two-way mirror. They were spaced out roughly fifty feet apart, and they were used to call management in case something suspicious was occurring. From the catwalk, one could easily see down each aisle, but customers on the floor could not see up onto the catwalk.

Periodically, we would send managers or other trained personnel to the catwalk if there was suspicious activity going on in the store. Catching shoplifters was not easy with that era's technology, though. Today, with the use of surveillance cameras, it's not as difficult to catch a thief, and so much easier—and safer—than walking the catwalk.

Workers' compensation is a type of insurance coverage that business owners must purchase to compensate employees who are injured on the job. In 1990, one of our store's cashiers developed carpal tunnel syndrome from repetitive motion in the wrists; the condition causes severe pain. While she was eligible for workers' compensation benefits, it was suggested to her that, rather than having surgery, she rested the injury and took on a different position at the store while her wrists healed on their own.

With a little coaxing and some training, I was able to convince the cashier to spend shift time on the catwalk, reporting shoplifting activity. You had to trust the person you allowed up on the catwalk. They were your eyes, watching the store, and that was extremely important.

This lady was middle-aged, super nice, trustworthy, and very religious. She was reluctant to do surveillance at first, as she felt she was spying on people. After some time, though, I think she realized she was catching people who were not doing the right thing—people who were stealing.

In her first year, she identified eighty-six individuals who were shoplifting. She would see suspicious activity and page me or another manager and tell us what she was watching or what had just happened. This cashier gave an accurate description of the person, allowing us to apprehend the shoplifters before they left the building. In the roughly three years she worked surveillance, our cashier-turned-sleuth identified over two hundred shoplifters and saved the store thousands of dollars in lost revenues.

This cashier would make her own hours, sometimes a few hours in the morning, sometimes a few in the afternoon. Never at night and never on the weekend. She reported to whomever oversaw the store that particular day, and up to the catwalk she would go.

She made the most memorable catch while working a morning shift.

She had checked in with me and headed about her business—walking back and forth along the catwalk, looking up and down the aisles. Most of the time, she was stationary, watching the HBA aisle. At the end of it was an endcap that had cartons of cigarettes on it. This was the aisle to watch, as most of the shoplifting in the store happened in this area.

On that morning, I was paged to call the catwalk. The cashier told me that there was a lady in the cereal aisle, filling up bags with groceries. There was a rack of bananas there, and she was tucked up against the rack, partially out of sight, filling her bags with groceries from the carriage.

The cereal aisle was directly across from a store exit. I was at the front-end phone and saw the lady heading for the door. With a little help, and no struggle, the lady was stopped, questioned, and on her way to the office. The female office manager came upstairs with us.

The police were called and were on their way. The shoplifter had stolen $99.31 worth of groceries.

As the catwalker was punching out to go home after her shift, I was in my office and asked her to come up. "Nice job," I told her, as I had on many other occasions. "Why were you watching the cereal aisle?"

"I was watching the HBA aisle, and God told me to go to the cereal aisle," she said. "Then, I saw the shoplifter filling up her bags."

Honest to God, that's the truth as she told it to me.

Chapter 8
The Only One I Got Wrong

The angel in the catwalk wasn't always right, and that taught me a valuable lesson about confronting shoplifters. I learned it the hard way the following year.

My angel in the catwalk had called to tell me a female customer put a disposable camera in her pocketbook; these items were very popular in the eighties and nineties and were considered high-theft items.

The female in question was shopping with a male person her age. They were just finishing checking out when I approached them.

"Did you forget to pay for the camera in your pocketbook?" I asked the woman.

The man was taken back and asked the woman for the camera. She reached in and pulled it out.

"This camera?" the man asked. My heart sank. It was not in a package and did not appear to be new. "We brought this camera in the store with us." He was pissed.

I was flushed and excused myself to call the catwalk angel. "Did you see them remove the camera from the display?" I asked her.

"No," she told me. "I just saw it placed in the pocketbook."

I went back to the couple and apologized.

"What are you going to do about it?" the man asked.

I thought for a second. Noticing a case of sixteen-ounce cans of beer under their carriage, I said, "How about a free case of beer?" I don't think I even waited for his reply. I headed to the beer aisle, got a case, ran back to the front and put it under the carriage, on top of the other. "How's that?"

The man paused, nodded his head, looked at me angrily, and away they went.

I did not sleep well for a couple of weeks. I had a wife, two young children, a home, and a career. What if I was sued or lost my job?

This couple taught the angel and me we had to be more careful. We had to be absolutely sure of guilt when confronting a shoplifter.

This didn't mean I would just let them walk out. I would watch a would-be shoplifter, make eye contact. I would bag their groceries if I wasn't one hundred percent sure, hoping the shoplifter might be spooked and dump the shoplifted items.

The rest of my career, if I was not positive about a theft, I never confronted a potential shoplifter.

Chapter 9
Bringing Stolen Items Back

Many shoplifters steal items and try to bring them back to the supermarket. They hope to get a full cash refund or a gift card. This type of theft happened numerous times, and shoplifters were looking for the maximum return on that theft—one hundred percent of the value.

As a merchant, I thought it was difficult to assess whether a customer was legitimately returning stolen merchandise for cash because, in most cases, there wasn't a receipt with the item in question. Even if the customer was legitimate, was the item even purchased at our store? There were tough calls to be made, and there were also policies on returns. Most of the time, it was up to a manager's discretion.

On some occasions, a suspect would find a receipt in the trash or on the ground, enter the store, and collect all or some of the items on that receipt. The suspect would then go directly to the service center with the items. The shoplifter would present the clerk with the receipt and items just collected and ask for a refund. Hopefully, the clerk working the service center was paying attention.

If the clerk noticed the suspect came from inside the store, he or she would alert a manager. With the use of the surveillance system, shoppers' movements were easy to confirm. Most times, we asked the suspect to wait until we'd checked the video; the longer the suspect waited, the more nervous he or she got. Sometimes, they'd just leave the store.

We had the technology then to also use the receipt for confirmation of theft. If we suspected a scam, we could use the date-and-time stamp on the receipt, in combination with our cameras, to easily obtain a picture of the person who bought the items the shoplifter was trying to return. It was a quick procedure, and if the person waiting for the refund wasn't the person who'd purchased the stock, we'd print a picture of the legitimate buyer. The picture was used to show the shoplifter waiting for the refund who had, in fact, actually paid for the items. It was rather comical at times, and the shoplifter usually took off running.

One incident happened on a night I was working. A female came to the service center with five large Italian submarine sandwiches and two pre-packaged cold dinners. The female told the clerk that the bread in the sandwiches was dry, and she didn't want the dinners anymore. She said the stale bread had ruined her appetite. She did not have a receipt.

Because the amount was over five dollars, the service center clerk had to get a manager's approval before she could issue a refund. The clerk called me. I asked if she saw the customer come from the parking lot or from inside the store. The service clerk wasn't sure, and I told the clerk to tell the customer it would take her manager a couple minutes to investigate it. The customer decided to shop for a few things.

This was an easy case. Going back on video, I could see the female came into the store and went directly to the prepared food section. She picked out the five sandwiches and two dinners and then went straight to the service center. She did not bring them in from her car.

I printed some pictures to show the female her actions and waited for her to come back to the service center. She was rounding the corner to the service center with a carriage with some groceries in it when she saw me. She must have noticed the photographs I just printed. I was holding them in my hand.

She left the carriage and walked right past me out the door. I went back to the camera and got a shot of her getting in her car and the license plate. Because she had attempted to shoplift, all the information was given to the police.

Chapter 10
Changing Price Tags

If you change a price tag, covering a higher-priced tag with a tag for a lower-priced item, that, too, is considered shoplifting. More precisely, shoplifting by switching a price tag. This happens more than one might think.

If a meat clerk found a package in a case that was missing its UPC barcode, the package could be reweighed, and the price could then be tracked through our register system. The surveillance system was then used to identify who took the price tag off the package and confirm what higher-priced package it was put on. Sometimes, we were lucky enough to find the people while they were checking out.

Sometimes, cashiers could also detect that an item's price had been altered. These stickers did not look pristine but rather a little messy. The price stickers are difficult—and time consuming—to peel. Most times, you could also see the original sticker underneath the false price.

In such cases, the cashier would call the front-end manager to handle the situation. This type of crime was a rare occurrence because many cashiers did not detect the altered price tags, working as quickly as they did.

One day in 2019, the meat manager was filling the chicken case and noticed an older female trying to peel the price sticker off a package of chicken. He called me right away, and I was able to observe the incident on the surveillance camera.

After the older female removed the chicken tag, a second suspect, a younger female, came over with a large package of steaks. They both went down an aisle and proceeded to put the chicken tag over the tag on the much-higher-priced package of red meat. After I saw this, I called the police. The officer arrived, and we watched these shoplifters in real time on the surveillance system.

The group we were tracking also included an older male, probably the older female's husband, and he was oblivious to the crime that was occurring. An officer went out to his cruiser to wait for the suspects.

When the shoplifters reached their car, two police cruisers pulled up adjacent to their vehicle. I sent a manager out just in case the officers needed any help deciphering the tags in question. The police checked all the groceries and discovered there were two large packages of higher-priced meats with less-expensive price stickers on them. The total "savings" for the shoplifters was $59.92.

The younger female and older couple were not related but used the same Electronic Benefit Transfer (EBT) card, most often used by individuals receiving benefits in a federal food program. EBT cards look much like a debit card and have an attached pin number. They are nontransferable. In this case, the card belonged to the younger female, and perhaps the deal was that she would have been paid in cash by the older couple for her help and EBT card use.

Roughly fifty dollars was saved on the one hundred they spent. That type of crime happened far too many times.

The females were arrested and ordered to pay the difference in price. I also wrote a letter to the local Department of Transitional Assistance to share what had happened with the individual's EBT card in hopes that they might take it away, or at the very least, give her a stern warning. I never heard a response.

Chapter 11
She Didn't like Civil Recovery

I did not catch the shoplifter in this case. She was caught in 2018 by an associate manager the day I was off. The report was on my desk in the morning.

The customer was with a couple of teenage girls, more than likely her daughters. My associate manager was watching the camera and saw this lady put a package of expensive hair spray in her purse. She appeared to be doing a weekly shop. He watched her until she checked out. He had told me she did not seem like the shoplifting type, and she was surprised when he confronted her after she was done paying for her groceries.

He went through the proper protocols and asked her if she forgot to pay for the hair spray she had in her purse. She was a little hesitant and looked in her purse as if perplexed, and there was the hair spray.

Now, according to my associate manager, this woman had just moments ago retrieved her billfold from her purse to pay for the groceries. She did not see the hair spray at that time? She offered to pay for the product, and the manager asked her to come to the office. She asked why, and he said she could settle the matter there. She reluctantly accompanied him, and her daughters took the groceries to their car. The teenage girls did not come back in the store to meet up with what I presumed to be their mother.

The associate manager made sure a female office clerk was in the manager's office when they got there. They sat down, and the shoplifter was asked for her license.

"What for?" she asked.

"Because you concealed the hair spray and did not pay for it, and I need to write a report. This is considered shoplifting," the manager said.

His report stated the female became very agitated. "The store is making a mistake. You can't be serious," she said.

At that point, my associate manager said he could call the police, which apparently set off another tirade from the shoplifter. Had it been me managing this incident, I would have called the police right that minute. My associate manager continued to navigate the problem on his own, however. He was patient and explained to the woman that either he had to call the police, or she could pay civil recovery to the store.

"And what is that?" she asked.

He explained the law and told her she could pay; the police would not be called, and she wouldn't have to go to court for a misdemeanor shoplifting charge.

"What gives the store the right to do that?" she asked.

"The state does," said my manager.

The shoplifter reluctantly paid a minimal fifty-dollar restitution sum and left. She promised never to return to the store. She uttered the words on her own initiative. You hate to lose a customer because of their ignorance of the law, but that was her choice.

Now, if this shoplifter had not gone into her purse to get her billfold out to pay for her groceries, it would be conceivable to think the incident could have been a mistake on her part. When I watched it play out on the surveillance camera footage, she did look around in her purse for her billfold at the register.

She must, then, have seen the hair spray. And how many people typically carry hair spray in their pocketbooks? Likewise, I can't think of any possible scenario in which she would have placed the hair spray in there accidentally while shopping. You want to think the best of people, but it isn't easy.

In all my years as a manager, I never had any shoplifter sue the store, or myself, after a shoplifting incident. This hair spray shoplifter did not either. She presented her ID, signed the paperwork, and we had video of her placing the hair spray in her purse. She did not have much of a case if she planned to challenge.

Until April 6, 2015, the Civil Recovery Law in Massachusetts well-protected merchants, offering them not more than five hundred dollars for each shoplifting incident—regardless of the dollar amount on the stolen merchandise.

The legislature changed the law in 2015, and lowered the dollar value the merchant could recover. If the value of the property stolen was less than fifty dollars, the merchant could only seek damages of fifty dollars. If the value of the property stolen was between fifty dollars and two hundred and fifty dollars, the merchant could only seek damages up to two hundred fifty dollars. The merchant could only seek damages of a maximum of five hundred dollars for goods valued over two hundred and fifty dollars.

If the merchant did not adhere to the law's guidelines, they could be fined five hundred dollars.

The change in the legislation was part of a larger bill focused on organized retail crime in Massachusetts and gave power to police departments and the courts to fully prosecute these retail crime rings.

While Massachusetts lowered the dollar amount a merchant could get when applying the Civil Recovery Law, the state of New Hampshire legislature raised the dollar amount from three hundred dollars to four hundred, for all shoplifting incidents.

At that time, a Massachusetts senator was quoted in *Loss Prevention Magazine* dated May 26, 2015. "This is a balanced bill," Senator William Brownsberger, co-chair of the Judiciary Committee, said. "It should help protect the public from the costs of criminal organized retail theft, while making the civil legal system fairer to innocent people."

When referring to "innocent people," I hoped the senator was not talking about "innocent" shoplifters.

Chapter 12
Grab and Go, Quick Change

Grab and go, in the shoplifting sense, means filling up a cart as quickly as possible and exiting quickly, without paying.

In one such incident of this type in 2012, there were three people involved. While they may have liked to think of themselves as an organized crime ring, they were more like The Three Disorganized Stooges, with Curly played by a female.

Because they did not even have the wherewithal to appear casual nor pretenses that they were just typical shoppers, these three individuals could not have stood out any more than they did. One male suspect grabbed a shopping cart, and they all headed straight to the meat department, clearly on a mission. The female had a huge pocketbook, which also caught my attention.

They filled up a carriage to the top with steaks and roasts. They had nineteen packages of boneless choice ribeye steaks, eight packages of spareribs, a whole choice bottom round roast, a tenderloin roast, and four packages of tenderloin steaks, with total worth at $410.54. I was thinking they intended to sell these packages of meat to a local bar for cash to support their opioid addictions.

One of the male suspects briskly left the store. He went to get the car they all arrived in. The remaining male and female made their way to the front with the loaded carriage and looked for their opportunity to get out. We had them all still under surveillance, and we had even secured the license plate of the car, which was now parked in the fire lane. The police were called.

The two suspects still inside headed for an exit, and we were able to stop them. To my surprise, the male shoplifter accompanied management to the office without incident. He seemed very mellow—under the influence of something. The female suspect, however, did not cooperate and headed across the checkout towards the far door.

Seeing this unfold, the shoplifter in the getaway car took off.

Because the law gives store personnel the right to detain suspects while waiting for the police, we did try to stop the woman as she fled, but she continued resisting.

I had a new manager with me at this point, and I contemplated detaining her but decided not to make a scene; the police would soon be arriving, I was sure. Instead, the new manager followed her out the door and into the mall. He was told to keep an eye on her. She ducked into the ladies' room inside the mall, and my manager waited for her to exit.

The police arrived, and I informed them that the female suspect was in the women's bathroom in the mall. I also told them I had a manager watching her movements. An officer was sent to meet my colleague. The remaining officer arrested the shoplifter we had in the office. This officer also used the photograph we had taken of the trio's car with the license plate, and the driver was arrested sometime later.

The female suspect had been in the bathroom for over ten minutes. Other patrons had come and gone. Just about when the police officer waiting there was going to bring in a female officer to intervene, a woman came out of the bathroom. She walked right by my manager and the officer.

After a moment, the manager said, "Hey, wait a minute. That's her!"

The suspect had a huge pocketbook, which must have had a change of clothes in it. She had completely changed—even her hat. She was arrested. The story was in the next day's newspaper, in August 2012.

The shoplifter who went to get the car and later sped off was arraigned on charges of larceny over two hundred and fifty dollars, accessory before the fact, and accessory after the fact—the latter two charges for helping prior to the crime and afterwards. He was held on a five-thousand-dollar cash bail.

The suspect who tried to push the carriage full of meat out the door was only charged with a single count of larceny over two hundred and fifty dollars. His bail was set at one thousand cash.

The female shoplifter was arraigned on a single count of larceny over two hundred and fifty.

About a month later, I got a letter from the probation officer regarding the incident. As a special condition of release, the judge told the three suspects to stay away from the store.

Chapter 13
Teardrop Tattoos

One city store I managed had a couple of bars around the corner. Shoplifters tended to visit the bars after leaving our store to sell what they had stolen for cash. Typically, they were funding a drug habit.

For several days, we kept an eye on a male we suspected was going to steal. He was a big guy—just over six feet tall, built like a rock with two solid teardrop tattoos under his right eye. He looked mean and was a guy no one wanted to confront.

The guy never took anything that we could see, but he always came back. After a few days of visits from him, I watched him carefully. He had two packages of ribeye steaks from the meat department, held in the crook of an arm the way a student might hold a stack of books. The value of the steaks was about thirty dollars.

He approached the door but turned around, never quite making it past the point of sale. He disappeared down an aisle but never concealed the steaks; he just wandered from the back to the front. Was he looking for a ride? Was he spooked?

Finally, after ten minutes, he put the steaks in our rack that held brochures and flyers, positioned next to the door, and left.

Enough was enough. I headed out of the store with another employee. We were not going to chase him; we wanted to tell him never to come back. I was on the sidewalk, and he was across the fire lane, heading for a car.

He was a good ten yards away when I yelled at him, saying, "I know exactly what you are doing, and you are not welcome back here!" I took a few steps off the sidewalk, and the guy turned around.

I threatened to call the police if he ever returned.

My associate grabbed my arm and pulled me back onto the sidewalk. I didn't know why he was pulling me, but I was done talking to the suspect by then.

"Why did you pull me?" I asked my colleague, once we were back in the store.

"The guy pulled a knife and had it in his hand," he said.

I didn't see it, but I thought it best to call the police.

The officer arrived, and I showed him a photograph of the shopper from our camera footage. The officer recognized the man and told me he was "bad news."

My associate asked what the teardrop tattoos under his eye was. The police officer said they were gang-related, a mark that indicated he'd spent time in prison. Our guy had a record, but the officer didn't elaborate. I was just thankful no one was hurt and thanked the police officer for coming so quickly.

I did a little research on the teardrop tattoos, but there were many different theories as to their meaning, differing in each region of the country. To further the confusion, open teardrops and teardrops that are full of color have different meanings. Teardrop tattoos next to the eye usually represent loss—possibly even the mark of a murder. An open teardrop tattoo can mean revenge is coming.

We were fortunate the suspect did not steal from us, and also fortunate that a week or two after his last visit, the responding officer came to tell us the teardrop offender had been incarcerated again. We didn't expect to see him for a while.

During my lengthy career, neither I nor my staff were ever physically harmed while confronting shoplifters. Most shoplifters were cooperative. The ones that weren't were apprehended through following procedures, and, sometimes, strength in numbers was required. Always, we could count on the police.

One reason I was pleased I'd never been robbed is robbery—taking property unlawfully by force—carries another whole set of protocols to follow, and any amount of money is not worth compromising a person's safety, getting hurt, or being seriously injured.

Chapter 14
Finding a Room at the Inn

In the 1980s and '90s, I was summoned to court for almost every shoplifter who was arrested in the stores I managed. I or a member of my management team had to go to court and testify as to what occurred during a particular shoplifting incident. We were the witnesses to what happened.

I was in court dozens of times during those years, and it was not always exciting. After a few times, it seemed old, boring, and time consuming. It was also time away from the store. With the introduction of closed-circuit television—also known as video surveillance—in the early 2000s, there became less and less need to be present in court.

The videotape documenting each shoplifting incident that led to an arrest was given to the police. The district attorney used the surveillance in court as evidence. If there was damage to a product or store property, a letter with the dollar amount for restitution was also sent by the merchant to the district attorney. Often, the shoplifter pled guilty in court, paid restitution, if any, and he or she also paid a fine and was most likely put on probation. The person was then typically free to go.

Even if video evidence was presented in a case, there were sometimes reasons store personnel had to appear live before a judge. On very rare occasions, if the shoplifter pleaded innocent, I might have to go to court to substantiate the video. Sometimes a shoplifter just pleaded innocent, hoping I would not show up to testify, and he would be free to go. This occurred a handful of times.

In 2014, I was in court to testify in such a case.

The man had shopped in our store with a handled basket and exited without paying for the steaks he had in his possession.

Someone saw him leave, but by the time we put it together, he was out of the store and gone. We got a good photograph of him leaving, and it was shown to all members of management. It was too easy for this shoplifter, and I was sure he thought he got away with it. He would be back.

The very next day, about the same time, the thief was seen entering the building and grabbing a hand basket. He went back to the meat department and put as many steaks in the basket as it could hold. The shoplifter made his way to the checkout and never stopped. He headed for the door.

We were ready for him. There were three of us. I had the police called when he came into the building. Surprisingly, he didn't give us any trouble, and we headed for the office. The shoplifter was five foot six inches tall and kind of portly, and I suspected he wasn't going to be much of a problem. He was definitely under the influence of something.

When we got to the office door, he changed his mind about cooperating and started to resist. It took the three of us to keep him in front of the office door. It was tight quarters, but we never fell to the floor. The police finally arrived. The shoplifter was handcuffed, arrested, and away he went.

About a half hour later, the arresting officer came back and wanted to talk to me. Apparently, the suspect had recently been released from prison. He had been in for many years on an accessary to murder charge—a murder his brother had committed. I had to go to court the next day because the police did not want this guy back on the streets.

I showed up the next morning at nine sharp. I was excited. It was my first time in court in quite a while. I met with the officer, and he said to sit tight to see what was going to happen. After a couple of hours, I met up with the officer and asked him what was going on.

"We have to find him a room," he said.

"A room?" I asked.

"A prison cell," the officer clarified.

The officer and district attorney were working out the details to make this happen. Another prisoner would have to be set free to make room for our shoplifter. I was in court in case the shoplifter changed his mind and pleaded innocent, in which case, I would have needed to testify.

A room was found for our shoplifter, and it was indeed a prison cell. The police and the district attorney convinced the judge to lock the suspect up quickly, rather than releasing him back out on the streets. A little after noon, the arresting officer said I was all set to go.

Chapter 15
Pregnancy Test Kits

Pregnancy test kits came on the market in the late 1970s and were available in supermarkets as of the 1990s—when supermarkets turned into a substitute for a clinic, and the kits became yet another item that was stolen. These kits were also sometimes used immediately in my supermarket's public restrooms.

Most items stolen are concealed in their entirety, but not the pregnancy kits. It was a strange but familiar phenomenon to find the empty packaging in store bathrooms—where there were no cameras—or in an aisle; an employee would then report the crime. While we couldn't apprehend the shoplifter in the moment, we could use the security footage to backtrack and find the person who left the packaging behind.

In one such case in 2011, an empty test kit package was found in an aisle and reported by a store employee to a manager. Using the surveillance system, we determined who dropped it there and were able to get a good picture of the female suspect. This shoplifter also stole dental floss and candy on the same day; all were concealed in her puffy white jacket pockets.

About a month later, an employee spotted a female taking a test kit off the shelf and thought it looked like the same woman from the previous incident. The staff member remembered the woman's white puffy jacket.

I watched the suspect go about her shopping. She opened the test kit, dumped the packaging, and put the kit in her jacket pocket. She also managed to put Dove deodorant in her pocket too. This shoplifter was not done yet, though. She took four fancy air fresheners as well and managed to get them all in her pockets.

The police were called, and the officer arrived before the suspect went through the registers. While we waited in my office for her to check out, I showed the officer the previous incident footage. He agreed, and confirmed it was the same shopper. I had already decided to have this female arrested and issued a "No Trespass" order.

While we waited, she did buy some groceries and had just finished paying for them when the front-end manager asked the female suspect if she forgot to pay for the air fresheners. You only need the suspect to admit to one item concealed. Allowing them to think we didn't know the full scope of their crime kept them calm and co-operative. The rest of the stolen items could later be revealed in the office.

This shopper acted surprised, saying she had forgotten she had the air fresheners on her person and wanted to pay for them. The shoplifter and the front-end manager walked to the office.

The officer on hand in my office did not wait at the register to question and arrest this suspect himself because his presence at the checkout may likely have caused the woman to flee or dump the items somewhere. If she'd emptied her pockets before she checked out, we could only get her for damaging the test kit.

Once in the office, the shoplifter was surprised to see the police officer, who told her to take a seat and empty her pockets. Out came the pregnancy test kit, deodorant, and air fresheners, and she placed them on my desk. We had already retrieved the pregnancy test kit packaging after she'd emptied and dropped it.

"This is my first time stealing," she told the officer.

He produced a photograph of her shoplifting the month before, when she'd taken the pregnancy test kit, dental floss, and candy. He received a blank stare from her. The officer arrested her, issued the no-trespass edict, then took her out to the police cruiser for a ride to the station.

A second officer arrived later to take our statements. I told him we would have to draft a letter to the district attorney for restitution from the previous incident and this one as well. The officer asked us to create a video of both incidents, so he could use them in court if needed.

About a month after the second arrest, the store received a check from the court for $41.51, which covered both shoplifting incidents. I never saw this shoplifter again.

Chapter 16
Parents Shoplifting with Their Kids

I almost lost my mind in the store in 2011 with a female shoplifter who had her newborn baby in tow in a car seat carrier attached to the baby seat of the shopping cart. The woman had a rather large diaper bag in the carriage, and the clerk who worked in HBA noticed this female acting suspicious and reported it to a manager.

The manager called me, and we watched the shopper from the office. She was definitely a high-end-products shoplifter and proceeded to put Alba Botanica, BioSilk Silk Therapy, Rusk, and It's 10 products in the diaper bag.

She took nothing for the baby.

After approximately fifteen minutes, the woman released the car seat from the baby seat of the carriage. The car seat had a handle, and the baby was in the car seat. The shoplifter put the diaper bag over her opposite shoulder and headed out of the aisle. As she passed the register, I asked her if she forgot to pay for all the beauty products in the diaper bag. She tried to sidestep me, and I blocked her way. My assistant store manager was with me as well.

The shoplifter was very argumentative and would not come to the office. As I tried to get her to cooperate, my assistant held on to the baby carrier, in which sat the baby. My assistant was focused on the child.

The shoplifter did not want anything to do with us and continued to try to get around us. I grabbed the diaper bag and the shoplifter yelled, "Leave me alone!"

At this point, my assistant looked at the shoplifter and yelled at her, "The baby!"

This seemed to settle the shoplifter down, and she stopped struggling. She came to the office with her baby in the carrier, diaper bag over her shoulder.

I motioned with my hands for the service manager to call the police. The female clerk came to the office, and the female shoplifter sat down and put the baby down next to her. The suspect gave me her license and had a disgusted look on her face.

I asked her to place the items she had taken on the desk, and she removed them. The total she owed the store was $149.58; $34.79 of that total was for the It's a 10 hair product alone.

Two police officers arrived and were briefed on the situation. One officer was as mad as I was at the woman's selfishness. You could see his anger on his face.

"Where's the baby food? Where are the diapers?" he asked.

One of the officers indicated to me that they could not take the baby back to the station to process the mother.

"I want her arrested nevertheless," I told him. "Do what needs to be done to make that happen."

The shoplifter was asked who could pick up her child within a half hour. "If there is no one you can call, we will have to call child services," an officer said.

The baby's father was called and arrived about forty minutes later and took the child out of the store. The one officer that remained cuffed the shoplifter and took her to the police station.

There were hundreds of incidents over the years in which parents stole in the presence of their children as well as many incidents in which the parents and their kids stole together—like a sport.

I had one incident involving a mother-daughter team. The daughter was ten or eleven years old, and she and her mother stole $81.37 worth of health and beauty items. Not one food item.

We went up to the office together, and I was going to call the police. The woman pleaded with me not to call them. She had a driver's license, but I got the feeling she was in the country illegally. After a lot of tears, I agreed to civil recovery. No police. The daughter waited downstairs, but she must have heard her mother crying. Very sad situation.

In yet another mother-and-daughter incident, the daughter was nineteen and had concealed in her large purse $41.19 worth of miscellaneous groceries, all under the watchful eye of mom. The daughter had steaks, deli meats, travel-size health and beauty aids, Kraft mac and cheese, and Pop-tarts. Not what the average kid would steal.

The mom went to the register with what groceries she had in her carriage. The daughter cut through. We asked her if she forgot to pay for the stuff in her pocketbook. A staff member took the teen to the office, and when mom was done checking out, she asked if she could join her daughter in the office as well. She could not believe her daughter had stolen.

We knew this was BS, as we'd watched them work together on the cameras. However, the daughter was caught with the goods, and not the mom. The mom paid the restitution, and away they went. They were not allowed back into the supermarket.

Sadly, there are many more stories of parents shoplifting with their children—each a little different than the other, many with infant babies. Diaper bags were always the thing to watch. Each unique circumstance was handled on an individual basis.

If the parents stole food, I would usually offer civil recovery, thinking the motivation was hunger. I knew civil recovery would be a hardship on the parent, but I wished to save them the penalty of court fines and the embarrassment. On some occasions, I would even let them go and direct them to a food pantry.

If parents were stealing to resell items, perhaps for drug money, or the items were not food-related, I called the police to handle the situation. No empathy. They deserved to be punished and embarrassed. First lesson for the children on right and wrong.

Chapter 17
Grand Larceny, Shopping Cart Full of $$$

Larceny and grand larceny charges are self-explanatory. Grand larceny is a lot grander than larceny.

In each crime or shoplifting event, there is a dollar amount associated with the incident, and when the amount exceeds a limit set by the state the incident occurs in, the crime becomes grand larceny. Grand larceny carries higher penalties, possible jail time, higher fines, and a felony record. Larceny is usually considered a misdemeanor with lighter fines, and the suspect generally receives probation.

In 2018, the Massachusetts legislature raised the dollar amount for grand larceny from two hundred and fifty dollars to twelve hundred dollars. I saw the change as a good example of not thinking the bill through.

Other amounts were considered. One thousand. Fifteen hundred. Nine district attorneys wanted a seven-hundred-and-fifty-dollar cap, but the legislature settled on twelve hundred. The twelve-hundred-dollar amount is not attainable for a shoplifting incident in a supermarket. A shoplifter could now go into any retail store and walk out with two fifty-inch TVs or two table saws worth five hundred each, and only be charged with a misdemeanor carrying no record. It didn't make sense.

In a supermarket, it would take three full shopping carts to even get close to the new grand larceny cap. That made stealing a shopping cart full of groceries a misdemeanor. This was totally wrong, and quite frankly, unacceptable.

Before the new legislation was voted into law, the Retailers Association of Massachusetts (RAM), representing thousands of retailers and business owners across the state, issued an opinion.

"Massachusetts retailers already experience large losses due to shoplifting, estimated at a billion dollars annually," the RAM statement said. "Most of these losses are attributed to professional criminal activity, from low-risk, high-reward, due to the already weak shoplifting laws. The new law for grand larceny (passing in 2018), further weakens our justice system and allows professional criminals and repeat offenders to steal more, avoiding the risk of higher penalties."

I have no desire to see a young person or a first offender receive a felony record, but the new law reduced the risk that the professional criminal would see any kind of serious punishment. The twelve-hundred-dollar threshold is higher than most states in New England. The threshold is also one of the highest in the country.

Senator Sonia Chang-Díaz, a Jamaica Plain Democrat and longtime proponent of many of the changes in the package, saw things differently than I do. "It's a huge historical turning point for our state when you set it in the context of the last several decades," Chang-Díaz said in an April 4, 2018, article in *The Boston Globe* written by Joshua Miller. "It's not a panacea. There are things we need to continue to work on, but it is a momentous, momentous occasion for the state."

Making it nearly impossible for a merchant to make a charge of grand larceny stick was not momentous to me. The law was passed despite feedback against it from RAM, district attorneys, merchants, and police unions. It was shameful the government did not listen or heed the warnings. The floodgates opened for retail crime in Massachusetts.

Grand larceny is now nearly unattainable in that state, so big-time shoplifting is almost worth the risk. The legislature wanted tough-on-crime measures reversed, and they did just that, softening penalties.

When a criminal does exceed a value of twelve hundred dollars in stolen goods, punishment is not more than five years in state prison, or a fine of not more than twenty-five thousand dollars and imprisonment in jail for not more than two years.

In a grocery store, it is indeed difficult to reach the cap for grand larceny, but a shoplifter can get close. One case I witnessed that carried the largest dollar amount stolen in one incident happened so quickly that, if I'd bent down to pick a piece of paper off the floor, I would have missed it.

I was at the service center, finishing up with a customer, when I turned to head towards the checkout. I saw a man with a carriage full of unbagged groceries skirt the express line and head toward the door. He held a Dunkin' Donuts iced coffee in his hand. Did I just see what I saw? I headed after him.

As I walked by, I asked the young cashier who was on the express lane if she saw what I saw. She didn't say anything. I think she couldn't believe what she had witnessed herself. I moved quickly to the exit and through the vestibule, catching up with the shoplifter in the fire lane.

As I grabbed his carriage, a twelve-pack of Red Bull energy drinks toppled to the pavement from the rack under the carriage.

"You need to pay for these groceries," I told him. His response was to bend down and put the twelve-pack back on the bottom of the carriage. He did not say anything and began to walk away.

I was in the middle of the fire lane with no back-up from the store or police officers to help me. The carriage was overflowing, and there were more Red Bull twelve-packs on the rack below.

The shoplifter was moving rather quickly away from me, and I stayed with the carriage. This was a my-bad moment. My thoughts were on the carriage, but in hindsight, it wasn't going anywhere.

I wish I had followed him and at least got his license plate number. Instead, I brought the carriage full of groceries back in the store. The police were called, and an officer showed up within minutes.

"How much," the officer asked, staring at the carriage.

"That has not been determined yet," I said. "I wanted you to see all these shoplifted groceries."

The carriage was taken to an empty register, and each item was scanned to get a total. Surprisingly, there was no red meat, rib eye steaks, or other typical high-end items. What the carriage did contain was items drug addicts don't usually shoplift: Six packages of boneless chicken breast, twenty-three packages of kielbasa, nine two-pound bags of shrimp, five packages of salami, ten jars of Cheez

Whiz, five cans of Café Bustelo coffee, eight twelve-packs of Red Bull, four packages of Pampers diapers, six packages of miscellaneous deodorant, and three packs of Gillette razor blades. The grand total was $633.73. Amazing.

It was determined that this shoplifter was stealing to replenish the shelves of a convenience store, possibly a bodega, as there were many in the big city close by. There were so many mom-and-pop stores in the surrounding area, it would have been very hard to find which one the suspect may have represented.

The local police department did a great job investigating this incident, however, at this writing the shoplifter has not been caught. Officers came and watched surveillance of the incident. The shoplifter had some tattoos, but he was not on the Massachusetts Most Wanted website or the local police department's Facebook page, so police could not identify him.

I was never good at makes and models of cars, and I wasn't much help to them in identifying the vehicle I saw—a small, black SUV.

At the time of this event, in 2017, if the shoplifter was caught, he would have been charged with grand larceny over two hundred and fifty dollars. Today, this shoplifter would only have been charged with larceny, a misdemeanor, and most likely he would have been fined, put on probation, and set free.

I object to that. This was not a young, wayward kid; it was a professional shoplifter. The Massachusetts state legislature got this new law wrong.

The passage of the grand larceny bill only hurt innocent people, and ultimately, customers will have to pay for it, not the state. The only people who benefit from the measure are the criminals themselves.

Chapter 18
Christmas Greeting Cards

Why would anyone steal $322.79 worth of Christmas cards? That's seventy-five cards at three to four dollars each, along with a dozen miscellaneous health and beauty items. Perhaps that shoplifter was selling the cards online?

This incident happened the week after Thanksgiving 2009, when I was on vacation. That week was a big vacation week in the supermarket industry—a refresh from the last holiday and recharge for the upcoming one, Christmas. My wife and I always went to an island, St. Somewhere, in the Caribbean. We would go with a group of managers and their wives for a well-deserved time of rest and relaxation. A report on the Christmas card theft was on my desk the Monday I returned.

Apparently, this female shoplifter was in the store on a Tuesday afternoon. She came in with a huge pocketbook. An assistant manager noticed her filling up bags she had brought in with her. She stood in front of the greeting card section and was very methodical about what she was choosing to put in her bags.

The manager in charge called the police. When the shopper was all loaded up, she laid her big pocketbook across the bags she had just filled up. She went to the checkout and bypassed the registers, but she was stopped at the door. Moments later, the police arrived, and the shoplifter was arrested. The assistant manager did not tell the police officer about a similar incident that happened ten days earlier. He had yet to realize this perpetrator was the same person.

The Monday after I got back from vacation, I saw that they caught this shoplifter. She was definitely the same woman who got away ten days ago. In that first incident, she took just health and beauty aids, many of them. The beauty aids were in small packages, and it was hard to pinpoint what precise products they were and what their value was. Loss prevention created a video for police. Our guy from loss prevention asked us to seek two hundred and fifty dollars in restitution for the first incident.

The judge didn't buy it. He dismissed the prior incident, and the store did not receive restitution. The female shoplifter did get charged for stealing the Christmas cards, grand larceny over $250, and she was permanently no-trespassed from the supermarket. I didn't see her again.

Chapter 19
Shirtless Crook

It was a raw fall morning in 2007—overcast and no sun. Not quite coat weather, but sweatshirt or lots-of-layers time. In the fall and winter, there are more places to conceal items—in jacket pockets, pouches of sweatshirts, etc. So, I preferred summer for catching shoplifters; it was easier to see the stolen items on a person.

This story is my favorite Sweatshirt Incident. A young adult male was seen leaving the store quickly by the front-end manager, who reported him as suspicious.

The manager got in touch with me, and we went to the camera room to see what the suspect had been shopping for. When playing the video back, we saw the young man had taken a hearty breakfast—a couple egg sandwiches from the prepared food hot plate, a small orange juice, a small milk, and a candy bar. He put these items in the pouch of his gray, hooded sweatshirt and left the store without paying.

This wasn't enough of a loss to bother the police with. I simply kept his picture in a file. We would keep an eye on him if he ever came back.

The same day, around twelve thirty, the front-end manager noticed the same young adult male, wearing the same gray, hooded sweatshirt. He called me to let me know, and I watched the suspect on the camera. He headed back to the prepared food area and took a hot sub and soda and ducked down an aisle to put the sub and soda in his pouch. The young man headed across the front, and more than likely was headed out the door without paying.

The front-end manager and I were at the door to greet him.

"Did you forget to pay for your sub and soda?" I asked him. "How about this morning's breakfast?" I did not have time to size him up because he was a runner. He made a dash for it, trying his best to get around us.

His sweatshirt came off in the struggle and then his T-shirt. Out the door he went. He got away. I called the police, and an officer responded. We showed him the video, and I said it might be easy to catch this guy since he was not wearing a sweatshirt or shirt on this chilly autumn day. He agreed, but the kid was never found.

We never saw him back in the store again either.

Chapter 20
A Little Help from a Meat Supervisor

Quite frequently, our store was visited by area supervisors to make sure we were doing what we were expected to do. Each supervisor was responsible for covering certain departments within the store—dairy, produce, meat, bakery, etc.

On one visitation day in 2013, I walked with the meat supervisor, inspecting the meat aisle, cutting room, storage areas, coolers, and freezers. After the visit, we were both at the front of the store, having a conversation about current employees. I was facing the first register, and the meat supervisor was facing the service center; he'd come up through the ranks and knew a thing or two about shoplifters.

While we were talking, a guy with a basket full of meat got in line at register one. It was a heavy basket, and the man kept trading hands to hold it. He was middle-aged with gray hair, wearing a T-shirt and shorts and looking a little rough around the edges. The supervisor and I stood about five feet from him. I am not sure he noticed us.

"Do you think this guy will make a run for it?" I asked the meat supervisor, whose back was to the shopper.

The supervisor turned to look at the guy, and as soon as he did the guy took off with the basket full of meat still in his hand. He was heading to the exit without paying.

I caught up to him in the vestibule. The automatic door slowed him up enough for me to grab a hold of his T-shirt, and that also allowed me to slow him down. With my other hand, I grabbed the belt on the backside of his shorts. The shoplifter dropped the red basket full of meat and then did his best to get away.

He pulled me through the vestibule and out to the sidewalk. The T-shirt ripped, and all I had was his belt. We were still on our feet when the meat supervisor caught up with us and got his arm around the suspect's upper body. We all managed to fall from the sidewalk into the fire lane.

I was still holding onto the shoplifter's waist and the meat supervisor had his arms. It was five o'clock, and a couple employees who were done for the day helped us. One of my full-time female associates was taking pictures of the incident with her cell phone, and I asked her if she could go into the store and tell the service center clerk to call the police. The shoplifter had stopped struggling, basically giving up.

The police arrived rather quickly, and the suspect was arrested. The total worth of the steaks in his red basket was $167.95. Nobody was hurt. No bones were broken. No scratches.

The officer would be back to get a video of the incident. I thanked the meat supervisor for his help, and we both went home for the night.

Chapter 21
Tattoo Tells the Story

Why does a person get a tattoo? Maybe the motivation is grief-related, gang-related, in service to our country, or maybe the tat has emotional relevance, or it's just fun. The funny thing about tattoos is, if you're a criminal, the authorities have one more thing with which to identify you. Police departments have files on criminals, and if you have a tattoo, that could be in your file.

On the Fourth of July, 2012, I was on vacation. As manager, I had top choice of vacation dates, and I always chose the week of the fourth. This one was a beautiful day.

Just before noon, a female was spotted bagging her own groceries and walking out of the store. The person who saw this, an employee, happened to follow the female suspect to her car, and she recorded a description of the car and the license plate number. The employee, who wasn't allowed to detain a shoplifter, called the assistant manager in charge of the store. My assistant manager called the police. It happened so fast that the female was gone before the assistant manager knew what had happened.

The police arrived. The license plate number and a surveillance photo were given to the officer, who gave my assistant an incident number and left. At the time, the surveillance photo was a frontal shot of the shoplifter entering the building.

When I returned from vacation the following Monday, I took time to look at this incident further. I always liked to investigate to see if I knew the customer. The dollar amount was well over three hundred dollars, and I wanted to see if there was anything else that might have been missed. I watched the video as the suspect bagged her own groceries in an aisle and proceeded to exit the building without paying. I then switched views to watch her come in and start her shoplifting.

The female entered the store, got a carriage, and passed by the entrance camera. It was a beautiful day, and the suspect had on a flowered, short-sleeved shirt. There on her right upper arm, just below the sleeve, was a recognizable, good-sized tattoo—three letters in a unique font. I thought about calling the police with this new information, but they had the license plate number, so I thought I should wait. Let the police do what they do.

Exactly thirty-five days later, and coincidentally another gorgeous day, it was mid-morning when the suspect entered the store wearing a plain white, short-sleeved shirt with the same tattoo visible. My assistant manager noticed her first and brought it to my attention.

The customer went only to the service center and was on her way out of the building. No shopping? I had the parking lot camera fixed on her while she stood on the sidewalk. She was talking with someone, and it didn't seem she was going anywhere soon. The police were called, and I gave the dispatcher the incident number we were given on the Fourth of July.

"That same suspect is here now," I said. The dispatcher told me an officer would respond.

When the officer arrived, I showed him the photographs of the tattoo from the Fourth of July and the surveillance photo taken that day. The police already had a video of the incident from the fourth. He agreed it was the same female suspect and headed out to the sidewalk, where the woman appeared to be waiting for a ride.

The officer confronted her and asked to see her right arm. The tattoo on her arm was the same as the picture from the Fourth of July. He told the shoplifter she was under arrest and handcuffed her where she stood on the sidewalk. She was escorted to the cruiser and took her place in the back seat—not the ride she'd been waiting for.

A month later, we got the letter from the district court's probation officer, letting us know this shoplifter was ordered to stay away from the supermarket and pay us three hundred dollars in restitution by March of the following year.

Chapter 22: Police Involvement

In working at thirteen different stores in my career, I was nestled in different towns with different police departments, in two states. Each police department had similar protocols for handling shoplifting cases. While the procedures varied from town to town, one aspect was consistent: All the police departments told me that if they were called to the store, they were there to make an arrest or write a summons to court—not to seek restitution for the store.

Upholding the laws on theft was their job, and we had success with police involvement much of the time. In a handful of incidents, the shoplifter escaped, and sometimes even then, the officer knew the suspect from a surveillance photo and was able to get him or her to return and pay.

Police officers did not respond to mediate. The judge would determine the fate of a shoplifter caught at the store.

Every police officer I came across acted professionally, even though their jobs are not easy—and they're not getting any easier. Criminals are getting the big raises from our lawmakers, in the form of legislation that has raised the cap on a grand larceny charge, a topic I discussed in Chapter 17. At the same time, there is a national movement to handcuff our police departments with defunded budgets.

In my tenure, police departments had two basic methods for dealing with shoplifting: issuing a summons for the shoplifter to appear in court or making an arrest.

If issuing a summons, the responding officer would gather the shoplifter's name and address and tell that person to expect a summons from the court. The officer would then file a complaint with the court, and if the court found probable cause, the shoplifter would receive the summons with a date to appear.

The police would also appear on the court date with the evidence against the shoplifter in hand.

Commonly, officers issued a summons if they felt the shoplifter was not a flight risk. During the COVID-19 pandemic, many police departments adopted this method as courtrooms were closed or not fully functional. The cases did not go away permanently, but they were postponed.

The second method police employed in stores I managed was to make an arrest. After asking store personnel for the details of the alleged crime and watching surveillance video of the incident, the officer would make a determination. He'd also ask the suspect to produce identification.

The officer would call all information into the police department to assess whether the shoplifter had outstanding warrants on other charges, or charges for failure to appear.

When shoplifters were arrested, they were often handcuffed and placed in the back of a cruiser. That was a judgment call. Some officers didn't use the cuffs.

I always appreciated watching shoplifters get handcuffed. I felt it sent a strong message to anyone watching, and I felt it made an impression on the shoplifter, too. However, in cases of repeat offenders, handcuffing had no apparent meaning to the criminal; it was just a formality.

Once in the back of a cruiser, the shoplifter was locked inside. They could not get out the rear door, nor could they access the front seat, where the officers sat.

At the police station, a custody sergeant or sheriff typically handled the booking: gathering name, address, and date of birth. The sergeant or sheriff also confiscated personal belongings such as cell phones, money, etc.

The officer would ask if the shoplifter understood his or her rights, and then the suspect would be photographed and fingerprinted. A decision was then made by the officer in charge on whether to prosecute the offender. Outcomes ranged from releasing shoplifters with a summons to appear in court, or if the shoplifter had outstanding warrants, holding the suspect at the station pending arraignment or bail.

I was arrested only one time in my life—for driving an unregistered motor vehicle. It was 1981, junior year of college, and I was pulled over for speeding by a state trooper. When the trooper ran my plates, my truck wasn't registered, which was an oversight on my part. The trooper handcuffed me and escorted me to the back of the cruiser. I remember the handcuffs were very tight around my wrists.

At the police barracks, I was processed. My fingerprints were taken, and my belongings were confiscated. I was placed in a cell and had to wait to be bailed out. It took over five hours for the bailsman to show up. Bail was paid, and my dad and I had to go get my truck, which had been towed and impounded.

Looking back, I remember being angry and upset. I was not mistreated in anyway by the troopers, but I resented the five-plus hours in a jail cell. Today, I realize it was my fault, speeding in an unregistered truck wasn't wise.

I wonder if shoplifters ever feel that same sense of personal responsibility while waiting in a holding cell?

Chapter 23
An Officer Points Out a Suspect

Typically, the police responded to our store after we suspected someone was shoplifting. In one incident in 2017, though, I got a call from an officer who noticed something was amiss.

He had just driven through the parking lot and noticed two males and a female at the far entrance of the supermarket. They had come from an adjacent parking lot—not ours. The three stopped before entering the store, seemingly in discussion. The officer thought it odd and called to warn me. Most customers headed right into the store to shop. The officer thought this discussion out front was some sort of planning session. He was right.

The officer suggested we keep an eye on these three persons. The officer and I knew each other well, given he'd responded to three dozen or more shoplifting incidents since I'd served as manager of that store. The officer's family also shopped at the store. He told me he was going to park on the side of the building and to give him a call if we saw something.

One of the males and the female looked middle-aged. The male had a bright red jacket that stood out, so they were easy to follow. This male and the woman came in the far entrance, took a carriage, and headed across the front aisle towards the service center.

The second male, who was younger, cut through the registers into the store. We lost him and stayed focused on the couple. They appeared to start a full shopping trip and were headed to the first aisle. My assistant manager and I took shifts watching the two as they made their way through the store.

Their interactions all looked fairly normal to me; my assistant agreed.

We watched the couple for about fifteen minutes when the police officer who'd called came in and sat down with us. With the police cruiser parked out of sight, he joined my assistant and me in my office. The three of us continued to watch the two people shop.

"We've seen nothing suspicious so far, except the male took his jacket off and put it in the carriage."

Within a few minutes, the male took some steaks and wrapped them in his jacket. He left the carriage, and the female, and headed to the far door where he'd entered, exiting through the registers and outside. He did not stop to pay.

The parking lot camera caught him walking to his vehicle in the adjacent lot. It was too far away to see exactly what he was doing, but soon the suspect had his jacket over his shoulder and was heading back to the store. No steaks. He entered the same way he'd exited and caught up with his female companion, putting his jacket back in the carriage.

The male suspect managed to make a couple more trips to his vehicle with shoplifted items wrapped in the jacket. We watched all these actions.

Meantime, the female was loading all the deli meats that had been in the baby seat of the carriage into her pocketbook. The couple then proceeded to the register to pay for the items they hadn't stolen.

While they waited in line to check out, the second male caught up with them. He got in line, and this younger male paid for the groceries the couple did not steal using his EBT card. We assumed this trio was not related, so the young man should not have used his card to pay for the couple's groceries.

The transaction enraged the officer. "They're getting groceries free and stealing on top of it," he said, leaving the office to get back in his cruiser.

The officer caught up to the shoplifting threesome at their vehicle. Another cruiser also arrived, and the trio was arrested.

Coincidently, the couple had warrants out for their arrest, and since it was a Saturday, they were jailed for two nights, until they could be arraigned by a judge on Monday morning. The total the couple tried to take was $158 worth of food.

The younger male's role was to provide his EBT card; we all suspect he would have received cash from the couple for paying with this card.

Because the shoplifters had to spend the weekend in jail, the sergeant asked if I would hold the groceries the shoplifters had paid for in one of our refrigerated coolers. This was a rather unusual request, but I complied.

Monday morning about eleven, the male suspect with the red jacket was at the service center to pick up his groceries. The full carriage was brought to him from the cooler.

"You can never come to this store again," I told him.

"Yeah, I've already been told that," he said.

Chapter 24
Bubble Gum Theft in a Duffel Bag

I had never seen someone shop with a duffel bag before. In 2014, an associate manager pointed out to me a suspicious guy who had entered the store and was shopping with a duffel bag in his carriage. Too big for the gym, the bag was one you could pack clothing in and sling over your shoulder. I watched this guy closely. He was five feet eight inches tall, medium build, wearing a T-shirt, jeans, and sneakers.

"This guy could be a youth sports coach," I imagined. "He could have just come from a workout or a practice."

The man headed down the gum and candy aisle as I watched.

When he got to the gum section, the shopper began putting ten-pack packages of gum into his carriage. Not just one kind but a good variety of flavors and brands—Juicy Fruit, Doublemint, spearmint. There were ninety-three packages in all. He almost cleaned all the inventory off the shelf in the process.

After he was done loading packages of gum into his carriage, he went to an empty aisle and began filling his duffel bag with the gum. This took a couple minutes.

When the bag was full, the man left the carriage in the aisle and headed towards the exit. On the way down the aisle, he took out his cell phone and pretended to talk on it. I stopped him at the door.

"Are you going to pay for all that gum you have in your bag?" I asked him. He looked surprised he'd been caught. He couldn't find any words. Finally, he said he left his wallet in the car and was going to get it.

I took the duffel bag and told him my associate manager would go with him to get his wallet. I know the story was untrue, but I played along. My colleague and the shopper walked through the vestibule, and when the last door opened, the suspect took off. My associate manager went after him, but the shoplifter had a good start and was unreachable. The suspect ran across the parking lot and around the mall, out of sight.

My associate manager and I wondered what that man was planning to do with all that gum? Resell it? This incident was a first for me. It was one thing for a kid—or even an adult—to steal one pack of gum, but ninety-three ten-pack packages?

At a vacant register, my associate manager and I dumped the contents of the bag on a belt. Along with the gum, the bag contained United States Postal Service mail, more precisely a Comcast cable bill with a name and address on it. Had to be our shoplifter.

I didn't think I would be calling the police, but with this information, I was able to make a report. We also had a surveillance photograph of the shoplifter for the police in case the bill was not his, unlikely as that was.

The police arrived, and the officer collected information, the photo, gym bag, and a cable bill. The gum had a retail value of $152.10. The officer seemed uninterested or almost bothered to be at the store. He gave us the gym bag back and kept the Comcast bill. I was not given a case number and never was informed if the case was resolved. There was nothing in the papers.

For misdemeanor crimes, there is a six-year statute of limitations to file charges. Once that six-year period is up, you can't prosecute. At this writing, the Gum Thief could no longer be charged for the crime. However, we did stop the gum from leaving the store, which is always a small win.

Chapter 25
Pecans for Pie

Holidays are a tough time of year for many families, especially for senior citizens, so there is always an uptick in shoplifting. The seven days leading up to Thanksgiving and the seven days before Christmas are the busiest days of the year. The sales volume is more than double that of any fourteen-day period during the rest of the year. Double volume means double foot traffic, which leads to more opportunity to steal.

Holidays are a festive time and can put financial strain on families. Jon Hurst, president of the Retailer's Association of Massachusetts says, "Just in general, stealing, theft offenses have historically gone up during the holiday season." Whether it's persons "stealing for themselves or stealing to make a profit, because more people are looking to buy goods, obviously, during the holiday season."

Understandably, shoplifting cases that happen during the holidays can be more poignant and tend to bring a tear to the eye—like this one.

Before Thanksgiving 2011, the store was busy. The place was decorated, festive, stocked, and ready for holiday shoppers. A manager noticed an older woman in the baking aisle put a bag of pecans in her purse. He alerted me, and I had someone keep an eye on her while she finished her shopping. I was told that she was at the checkout and that the pecans were still in her purse. The manager did not see the lady take anything else.

I was absolutely not going to have her arrested, but I also wanted to speak to her about stealing, even though she was older than me. We did not go to the office, but I pulled her aside to talk. I quietly asked if she forgot to pay for the pecans she had in her purse. The old lady started to cry, and said she needed them for her pecan pie she was making for Thanksgiving. She couldn't afford to pay for them.

The front-end manager and I were moved nearly to tears. He was the fastest in offering to pay for the pecans. He opened a register, deposited his money, and handed the pecans to the woman.

"God bless you!" was her response.

"Happy Thanksgiving," we told her.

Her story is one of too many to count.

Chapter 26
Helping a Shoplifter Buy a Car

Stories of other shoplifters also tugged at my heart and made me act in ways I would not have suspected.

In 1984, I was an assistant manager in a new store. We'd been open for about a year when the manager hired a woman who recently moved to New England from the South. The new employee was the single mother of a six-year-old girl. She began to work in my department, in the grocery aisles.

After a few months, the woman had caught on and become a reliable worker. The store manager promoted her to full-time grocery clerk. The problem was she needed a car. I'm a nice guy, and I wanted to help.

I met her at the local Ford dealership, where I've purchased all my trucks, and I introduced her to the salesman. He was able to get her into a relatively inexpensive new car, financed with a three-year loan from Ford credit.

About a year later, I got transferred to another store and continued working as an assistant manager. I lost touch with the new full-timer from down South. A few years after that, I was promoted to manager and was assigned a store to manage, a new one at that.

Several years later, in 1990, there was an incident in the store with two people, a male and a female, attempting to shoplift nine cartons of cigarettes, then valued at about twenty dollars per carton. The male shoplifter tried to get away, and there was a struggle. The female shoplifter watched and didn't move.

I had been taking karate lessons for about six years when this incident happened and had recently earned my black belt. Everyone at the store knew I was taking lessons. During the struggle with this shoplifter, I got some help from the meat manager and another employee.

When the shoplifter was finally on the ground and detained, I was sweating and trying to get my breath. The meat manager asked me, "How are the karate lessons going?" We laughed until the police arrived not long after.

The town was a small one, and only one officer showed up. He arrested the male shoplifter and took him to the station. The female came to my office.

Both the man and woman were under the influence of some drug. The female was quiet. I asked her for her ID, and she gave it to me. I began filling out the paperwork for the incident. The police would be back to get her on a charge of shoplifting.

She finally spoke up, "You don't remember me?"

I looked at her and then at the ID, and no, I couldn't place her.

She said, "You helped me buy a car."

Then, I remembered her. It was a couple hour's drive and a state away when I last worked with the woman. The first name, on the driver's license, was what I remembered. The last name had changed; obviously, she had gotten married.

I know we had said a few things to one another after she started to talk, but I don't recall what was said—only that having known me in another era didn't help her case at all. The police officer came back and arrested her.

He gave me the information on the male suspect, her husband, and off to jail she went. I couldn't help thinking about her daughter, though. Where was she? How was she? She would have been twelve or thirteen.

The shoplifters pleaded guilty, and I didn't have to go to court.

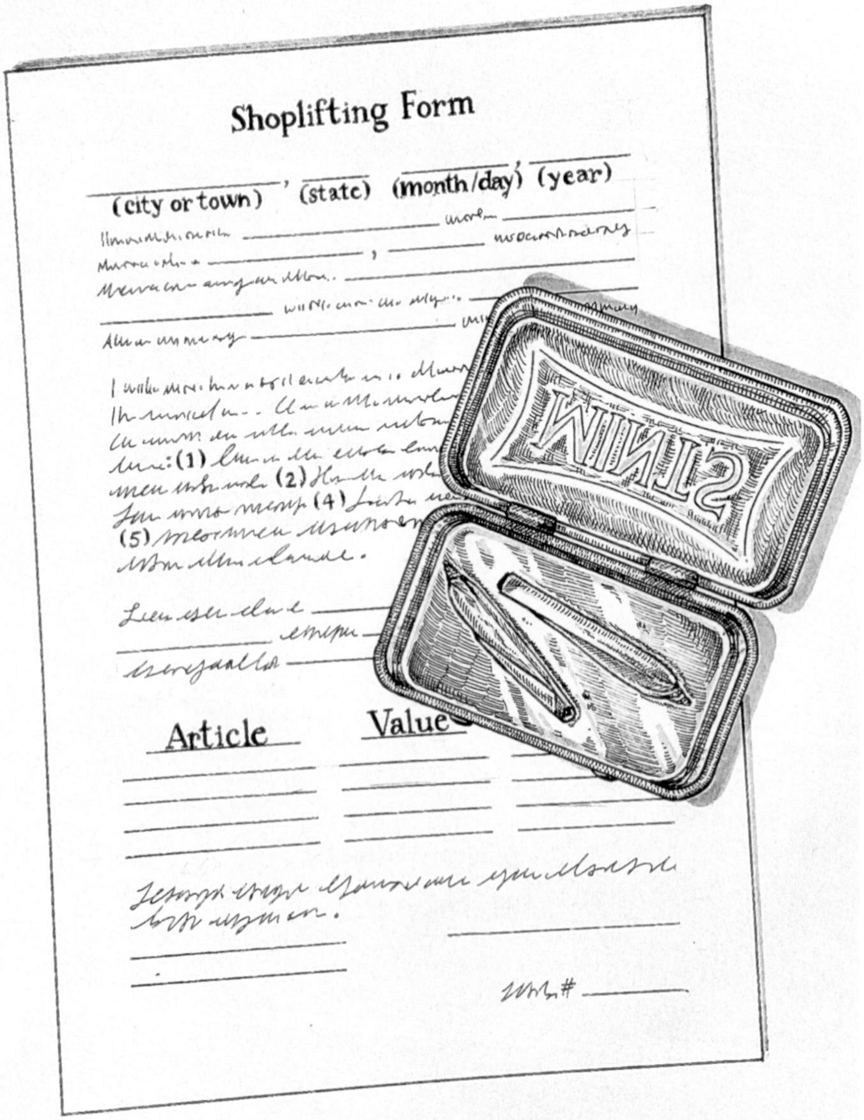

Shoplifting Form
(city or town)
(state)
(month/day)
(year)
Article
Value

Chapter 27
Joints in an Altoids Container

This is another sweatshirt story. I hate sweatshirts because they're loose and have pockets, and their bulk makes it hard to detect if there is anything hidden in them.

In 2012, a young male came into the store on a slow day. He was acting suspicious, looking around, and a manager noticed him. It was lunchtime, and two of us ate our lunches in the office and kept an eye on him. The young man kept looking around and went in and out of many aisles. He finally settled himself in front of the air freshener section. Taking his time, he tried just about every different kind of air freshener there was. It was entertaining to watch while having lunch.

He would do a quick spray and lean into the mist and smell. I guess he was looking for that certain odor. We had about finished our meals when the man settled on an air freshener he must have liked. Then, he got back to looking around and wandering in and out of many aisles.

Finally, he found an empty aisle, and with one last look, put the can of air freshener into the front pouch of his sweatshirt. The front-end manager left the office and waited up front for the shoplifter to come out of the aisle. The suspect walked part-way across the front of the store, through an open register, and he headed for the door without paying for the air freshener.

The shoplifter was stopped at the door, and the front-end manager asked him if he was going to pay for the air freshener. The shoplifter said he had forgotten.

Now, the product was a ninety-nine-cent item. If I called the police, they might have laughed at me for wasting their time. The front-end manager knew I would not call the police for this incident, but instead the young man's parents.

The shopper sat down in my office. I pulled out a shoplifting form, which we would fill out as I asked his name, address, and date of birth. His rights would be read to him under the so-called Miranda Rule. Finally, I would document what he stole and ask him to read and sign it.

The shoplifter was nervous, and I hoped I could scare him straight.

We went through the motions, and I told him even though the air freshener was only ninety-nine cents, I still would have to call the police. "Why are you stealing air freshener?" I asked him.

"I have a pet gerbil, and my bedroom smells bad," he responded.

"Did you take anything else," I asked. He had moved in and out of the aisles so quickly, I wasn't sure if he had anything else concealed on his person.

"No," he said, standing up and picking up the sweatshirt's pouch up and giving it a shake.

I noticed a bulge in the front right pocket of his jeans. I asked him if it was a cell phone. He said, "No." If he had said, "Yes," I would have told him to sit back down.

"Please show me what's in your pocket," I requested.

He reached into his pocket and pulled out an Altoids container. "Please hand it to me," I said. I wanted to be sure he had not stolen the Altoids as well.

He handed me the case reluctantly, and I noticed it was lighter than it should have been, like nothing was inside it. I opened the container. Inside there were two joints. I guessed then that the air freshener was to mask the smell when he smoked his pot.

My front-end manager said, "Guess we are going to call the police now." He was right. I had to call the police, and I did.

The police officer showed up, and I explained what happened. "Do you want to charge him with shoplifting?" he asked me.

"No," I said, thinking the possession of marijuana charge was the more serious of the two crimes. I was wrong.

It was 2012, and the state had changed its possession laws. It allowed for possession of minimum amounts of marijuana for personal use. The front-end manager and I looked at each other in amazement when we learned the young man was free to go.

Guess we should have been more up to date on possession laws. Ironically, if we had pressed charges, the shoplifter would have had to appear in court and at least be fined for shoplifting. I'm not sure whether it was a learning incident after all.

Chapter 28
Hostile Senior Citizen

There were thirteen stores I worked in over the course of my career. In November 2014, I was a recent arrival in a new town, in a new store. I was getting acclimated—learning the lay of the land, the vendors, local authorities, police, etc. These transitions didn't happen quickly.

About a month after my arrival, I was in my office, talking to an associate and watching the security camera at the same time. I saw an older man walking across the back main aisle of the store with a receipt in his hand. He was filling two reusable bags with what he had in his carriage. It looked odd to me, so I kept an eye on him.

He came to the front of the store and approached the courtesy booth. I thought maybe he planned to pay for his groceries there.

My assistant manager came up to the office and saw who I was watching. He had been at the store since it opened and said, "That guy is in here all the time. He also drives the senior bus."

Every Tuesday, the bus came to the store with about two dozen senior citizens out to do their weekly shopping.

As we watched, the man purchased two packs of cigarettes and headed for the door. My assistant and I looked at each other amazed and ran down the stairs to get him. This was the start of something very ugly.

"What is this about?" the man yelled as we walked him back to the office. Glaring at me, he continued to repeat, "You are going to be fired for this."

He did not want to cooperate and kept yelling at me, "I am going to own this store. You're going to be fired for this." He asked, "Where's the manager?"

"I'm the manager," I told him.

When I asked the service manager to call the police, the man said to me, "Now you're in for it." He never mentioned the receipt.

I had had just about enough of the guy, but I did feel a little uneasy. I had only witnessed him filling up his bags. I'd only been wrong once in my career, and this guy was adamant he didn't do anything.

I was anxious about his protestations, especially given it would be my first meeting with the local police.

As we waited, the shopper would not shut up. My assistant was in the security office, reviewing camera footage to make sure the man hadn't brought these groceries in with him, which was highly unlikely. But we had to be right.

The police showed up—two officers—and still, the man angrily proclaimed his innocence. He wanted me to be arrested.

"Quiet down," one officer told him.

My assistant came out of the back and nodded his head. I was relieved; the man had not brought the groceries into the store with him.

I told the officer what I saw, and they arrested the shoplifter. He kept hollering all the way to the back seat of the police cruiser.

The other officer stayed behind to get statements. He had the receipt that was in the man's hand and the one he received when he purchased his two packs of cigarettes minutes ago. The receipts were the same, same two packs of cigarettes, but the dates were different.

"What are the chances he did the same thing when he purchased the first packs of cigarettes?"

"Oh my God," I thought. "I like the way this guy thinks."

We went to the security office and watched the video for the previous date and time that was on the receipt, and lo and behold, the man had stolen groceries on the earlier date as well.

The service manager was able to trace how many times the same two packs of cigarettes were bought together. Loss Prevention was invited in to tally the full amount of goods stolen by this older shopper. It came to thirteen hundred dollars, and we drafted a letter to the district attorney, seeking restitution in that amount.

The store had been open for six years at that point. We suspected the man took far more over that time, but we could only go back so many months on the surveillance video.

We put all our findings and surveillance together and gave it to the police department. I talked to one of the arresting officers a week or two later to see how we made out. Apparently, the judge only put the man on probation. No restitution.

This was wrong, and I called and spoke to the district attorney.

"What did we do wrong?"

"You can't get blood from a rock," the DA told me.

Really?

The old man walked. The court got its fees, and we got nothing. Not fair, but there's more.

One year later, I was on the sales floor and saw the old man. I had to do a double take. I went to my office to find his photograph. It was him. He had lost a little vitality and seemed a little slower in his step. Definitely not as feisty.

Most everyone who is arrested and behaves inappropriately is ordered not to trespass on the property. The man had been told never to come back.

I caught up to him in the first aisle. I put my hand on his carriage and asked what he was doing in the store.

"The judge said I could come back after a year," he said.

"Do you have the thirteen hundred dollars you owe us?" If he paid us, I would have allowed him to shop again. Maybe.

"I can't pay," he said, so I asked him to leave. Never saw him again.

I have always been an advocate for senior citizens. I let many go when they shoplifted food or little extras from us, depending on each situation.

I talked to seniors about stealing and the consequences. "Let your conscience be your guide," was my favorite saying.

This man was different and difficult. He was hostile. He did not have my compassion or sympathy. I'm not sure he had a conscience either.

Chapter 29
Kleptomania and Habitual Shoplifters

According to the Mayo Clinic, kleptomania (klep-toe-MAY-nee-uh) is an impulse control disorder causing a recurrent inability to resist urges to steal items that one generally doesn't need and which usually have little value. It is a rare but serious mental health disorder that can cause emotional pain for the person who is affected and those they love.

I had known about kleptomania since I started work at my first grocery store. Working in a supermarket, I would often hear of someone stealing; the people we caught often were referred to as "kleptos."

When I became a manager, there were many incidents in which people stole items they didn't need, for no apparent reason. These persons who shoplifted had the money to pay for the items stolen. They could not explain why they stole. They were impulsive and sloppy shoplifters.

Kleptomania was often used as a defense for shoplifters of the wealthy class, during the late 1800s through the early 1900s. The individual, usually female, had the money to pay for the items shoplifted, but impulsively took the items anyway. Shoplifters using the kleptomania defense usually got off, or jail time was reduced. After all, they were facing a four- to five-year prison sentence. The less fortunate were not so lucky and were usually sentenced to prison.

During this time, it was almost exclusively women who were charged with shoplifting. One reason is that women did all the shopping. The other is they wore clothing that easily could conceal merchandise. Open almost any *The New York Times* newspaper during that era, and you would read exclusively about women who were caught and sentenced for shoplifting.

The hundreds of times I went to court, there was never a defense of kleptomania. Not because it didn't exist but because penalties for shoplifting in our era are minor—if the shoplifter gets charged at all. It's highly unlikely the shoplifter would face any time in jail. Mounting a defense for kleptomania today would be expensive, embarrassing, and unnecessary.

I did read up on the disorder to have a better understanding of it. Anyone I caught shoplifting more than once—and there were many—were arrested for the second incident. Even if these shoplifters wanted to pay civil recovery, after being caught that second time, I didn't allow it. I wasn't being punitive. I thought these people needed help, and I wanted to call attention to them.

I once caught a teacher from a local high school stealing a few items even though she had plenty of money with her. Once, I also caught an older woman stealing a spatula, paying minimal civil recovery, only to be caught two weeks later.

That woman arrived on the senior bus to do her shopping. The second time I had her arrested, her son came to visit me. He owned a successful business in a neighboring town.

"Why did you have my mother arrested?" he asked me.

"It was her second offense," I replied.

He didn't know it was her second time. "Why didn't you call me? You know me."

"I did not know the woman I was dealing with was your mom!" I said, adding, "She could definitely have kleptomania, and she might need help."

There is also a story of a little old lady, tiny, sixty-six years old. It was 2012, and a female associate manager spotted this shoplifter filling up bags in a spot that was out of camera view. She had come in with a carriage from the mall, not ours. She did not pretend to pay and headed out the door.

She was caught on the sidewalk and brought to the office. All the bags that were in her carriage were brought to the office. Not only were there groceries from our store, but candles from the candle shop in the mall. There were a number of clothing items from a department store with the price tags still on them. There were even more new items in the bags that were unrecognizable as to where they came from.

Hundreds of dollars' worth. All appeared to be for personal use.

My female associate manager thought the woman was a kleptomaniac. I agreed. The shoplifter sat there and said nothing. Because everything she'd stolen was for her own use, and not for resale, I didn't think she was a professional.

She had no way to pay for what she had. The shoplifter had no cash, credit cards, or checks with her. She couldn't pay for the $92.94 worth of groceries she stole. Why do you go shopping with no means to pay?

The shoplifter only had a state ID, no driver's license. We talked about civil recovery, but how would she pay? The shoplifter told me she had money at home and would send it to us. She didn't want the police called and neither did I.

My female associate offered to drive her home and bring her back to pay civil recovery. This was unusual, not procedure. The shoplifter wanted to buy the groceries she had shoplifted. She needed them to eat.

My associate manager took her home. The shoplifter lived right around the corner. I told my associate manager to stay in the car and not go into her apartment with her. They reached the woman's apartment, and the shoplifter went in to get her money. The shoplifter came back out, and the two drove back to the store.

She signed the paperwork for civil recovery and paid two hundred and fifty dollars. She paid for her groceries separately. She was helped outside for the bus to come to take her home. I called the three stores in the mall to tell them what happened and to come get their items that were stolen.

The next day a police officer showed up.

The manager of the candle store wanted to press charges. She had surveillance footage of the incident. The officer asked me if the store wanted to press charges as well. I told the officer that I settled with the shoplifter with the civil recovery law. I am pretty sure he did not know what I was talking about but asked me for her information. I gave it to him.

I am not sure what became of the shoplifter. I didn't see her name in the local papers, and I never saw her in the store again either.

While I am not a therapist, I believed shoplifters, stealing multiple times, should receive counsel. I would suggest to them they might talk to a minister, priest, or rabbi. Conversations with these types of persons are usually free and confidential. There are programs out there that can help.

There is, in fact, a twelve-step program for people with kleptomania. People who steal repeatedly and impetuously are generally remorseful, and ninety-nine percent of the time, they don't try to flee. They simply feel shame and humiliation. Help is available.

Chapter 30
McCormick Addiction

O ne afternoon in 2014, I caught a guy stealing McCormick extract—four one-ounce bottles still in their cardboard containers. The shoplifter put them in a reusable bag, which I watched him also steal as he walked across the front of the store.

He headed for the door, and I kept an eye on him until he moved toward the exit. We met each other in the vestibule, and I asked the shopper if he forgot to pay for the extract he had in his bag. He said he had and followed me to the office without incident. The shoplifter didn't want the police involved and agreed to pay civil recovery. He made restitution and left the store. I didn't give him a No Trespass order as he was cooperative.

"You may continue to shop here, but you can't steal from us again. When you steal from the store, you are stealing from all of us who work here."

Fast forward a couple months.

At the end of each night, the grocery staff broke down and tidied the grocery aisles, so they were neat and ready for the next day's customers. Any empty packages or damaged merchandise was brought to the attention of the closing manager.

Two nights in a row, employees found empty McCormick extract boxes on the shelf in the baking aisle, missing the bottles inside. The bottles are quite small and easy to conceal.

The first night, there were four empty packages, and the next night there were six. I did not think about the individual who I'd caught months earlier; he didn't cross my mind, perhaps because he'd taken the box with the bottle.

Two nights after the discovery of the empties, we found six additional empty boxes of extract. It was time to look at some video to see if we could catch our perpetrator.

Now, watching surveillance video for a particular moment in time can be daunting and tedious. It is not as easy as one might think. It can be done, but it is time consuming—and costly, which is why civil recovery feels so necessary to merchants.

While we weren't dealing with a major loss—the extract cost $2.99 a bottle—there was a pattern developing. We hoped to find the suspect.

The Monday before Easter Sunday, we discovered fourteen empty containers of extract. They were on my desk when I got to work that morning. All from the weekend.

I finished my morning duties and went to the security office to try to find out who was doing this. There was a stationary camera, watching the aisle where the spices were. I watched the film for about an hour, maybe more, and finally saw the guy who was taking the extract, all displayed on the bottom shelf.

I watched the shoplifter squat like a baseball catcher, open the boxes, and put the bottles in his pocket. He neatly closed each empty box and put it back on the shelf.

I went back to roughly the same time in each of the nights we found the empty boxes. It was the same guy each time. The video was not crystal clear, so it was hard to get a good look at his face. Each night, he took a few more bottles of extract than the previous night.

In total at that time, there were thirty-six missing packages of McCormick extract. We had what we needed to catch him.

I stayed late with another manager to catch this guy in the act. We set a camera that had the capability to pan, tilt, and zoom on the spice section. The guy who had been coming in every night showed up and went right to the spice section. He emptied one package of extract and put the bottle in his pocket. When he got to the next box, he was surprised by a cashier who was putting overstock back on the shelves.

"You shouldn't be doing that," she told him. I was never so proud of that sixteen-year-old employee for speaking up. The fact that she noticed what the guy was doing was wrong and said something about it was remarkable to me, and I later told her so.

She spooked the shoplifter, though. He took a second bottle and headed towards the door.

On my way out of the office, I told an employee at the service center to call the police. We had to move quickly as our suspect was rushing to the exit.

We caught him at the door, and I finally recognized him. He was the guy I'd caught two months ago. His hair was different, and he was better groomed.

"Did you forget to pay for the extract in your pockets?" I asked him.

This time, he was not cooperative, and he tried to get away. Another manager and I struggled with him, trying to detain him, and we ended up on the floor. The manager and I were able to hold him successfully until the police arrived, though.

The officer, who I dealt with often, asked, "What are these bottles?"

"McCormick extract," I said.

He seemed a little put out to be called for such a small item.

I explained that over the previous eight nights, this same suspect had stolen thirty-six bottles. He then was puzzled as to why someone might want to steal that much extract.

"They contain alcohol," I explained. "It's like drinking a nip bottle from the liquor store."

Our shoplifter needed professional help.

You can't make this stuff up.

Chapter 31
OTC Shoplifting High (Coricidin HBP)

Extract wasn't the only item on our shelves that could be stolen to get high. Coricidin HBP cough and cold syrup is an over-the-counter medicine that was also often stolen for that purpose, and many who snatched it consumed it in our public restroom before leaving.

Coricidin HBP contains dextromethorphan, an active ingredient developed to suppress a cough. Dextromethorphan, or DXM, when taken in large doses, can cause hallucinations, slow-motion sensations, feelings of intoxication, and just plain being high. Consuming it is often referred to as Robo-Tripping.

There are a few more over-the-counter cough and cold medicines that have dextromethorphan as an active ingredient. Another such medication is Mucinex DM. In most states, it's legal for anyone to purchase these medicinals. Slowly, though, states are requiring that buyers of products containing dextromethorphan be over the age of eighteen, and they must show an ID.

The grocery clerk who ordered and stocked medicine in our store noticed, in 2017, that the Coricidin HBP slots on our shelves were suddenly empty. It was never that fast a seller. We tracked shoppers' movement in that aisle, and there were many packages unaccounted for.

Around the same time, the maintenance department was finding empty packages in the restrooms, always two at a time. The clerk kept a close eye on the item and would report when it went missing.

One day, we got lucky and were able to photograph the suspect who was taking the medication and consuming it in the bathroom. At this point, there were eight empty packages in my office.

The suspect was in his mid-twenties, six feet tall, and of medium build. He usually came in the mid-morning but not necessarily on a regular schedule. A couple days after we got the photo of him, he was in the store, in front of the cough and cold section. We watched as he took two packages off the shelf and headed to the restroom. He came out a few minutes later and was met at the exit as he was planning to leave. The shoplifter came to the office without incident and appeared a little out of it. The police were called.

The officer arrested the shoplifter, and he did admit to stealing the other eight packages; I suspect there were considerably more than eight. We gave a video of the suspect taking the Coricidin off the shelf and to the restroom to the police. A letter seeking restitution for fifty dollars was also sent to the district attorney.

A couple months later, I saw the shoplifter in the store again, heading for the cough and cold section. Really, was this guy going to steal again? To my surprise he took two packages from the shelf, headed to the registers, and paid for the Coricidin HBP. He would do this now and then. This guy had an addiction and clearly needed help—along with another customer, whose medication of choice was Mucinex DM.

The Mucinex user was a middle-aged female. She also consumed two packages of medication per visit, on four different shopping trips. Empty packages were found in the restroom, and with a little surveillance, we were able to get a photograph of this female, but we did not apprehend her right away.

In the first three incidents, the woman was by herself and purchased groceries in addition to stealing the medication.

In June 2014, our suspect came to the store on a steamy day—this time with a male companion and a young girl, perhaps her daughter. We didn't recognize her right away because she wasn't wearing the sunglasses she typically had on. She was the right height though—just under six feet—and she was big-boned.

The surveillance photos from the previous incidents were checked against her appearance, and we were ninety-nine percent sure we were watching the correct suspect. I watched the trio as they shopped, and after fifteen minutes, I decided I was wrong. The three stayed together and even walked by the cough and cold section without incident. I was about to stop watching when the female suspect left the other two and stood in the medicinal aisle alone.

The female headed to the restroom with two packages of Mucinex DM. A little while later, she was back on the sales floor with nothing in her hands. She was wearing a tank top and shorts, no pocketbook. We had the restroom checked, and in the trash barrel were the two empty packages with all the pills missing from their holders. She was definitely the same female suspect we'd been tracking.

I decided I would let her family finish shopping. I planned to approach them at the checkout. My memory of this lady, still in my head, was that she stared straight ahead, like she was lost in space. The male with her finished paying for the groceries, and I approached him.

"Can we talk privately?" I asked. We both stepped aside, and I explained the situation. I thought the guy was going to explode—not at me but at his wife.

He thought for a moment and asked if I would let his wife and daughter go to the car, so he and I could go somewhere quiet to talk. I liked that idea. I did not want his daughter to see or hear what I was going to tell him.

The trio had two carriages of groceries, and the wife took one and I took the other with me. We headed to my office, but I still had it in mind that I was going to call the police. The woman had taken too many packages of the Mucinex DM. I knew, though, from watching the three of them shop, that there was no way the husband and daughter knew what the mom had done.

We got to the office, and I showed the husband all the empty packages. The surveillance photographs of his wife, taken on the dates we had been watching her, were laid out on my desk. He shook his head and told me he didn't think his wife was using the drug anymore.

"She has been talking to a doctor, to get better," he told me. "I will make sure that continues."

I then decided it was best not to get the police involved; I changed my tune. I truly believed this husband would help his wife get the help she needed. He paid for a number of packages, and he left.

I never saw them shop at my supermarket again.

Chapter 32
Little Girls Shoplifting Big Girl Things

When I caught young shoplifters, especially those under age sixteen, I called their parents. I believed the parents would take care of the situation. Most of the teen shoplifters were dropped off at the mall or the store to shop while the parents went home to do their own thing, or to shop separately in the store. However, parents were not called in the following incident.

One Thursday in 2010, two young girls entered the store about one in the afternoon. They stood out because it was a school day, and there wasn't anyone else their age in the store. A manager told me they were in the health and beauty aids aisle, and I watched them on the cameras. They moved around a lot in the aisle, looking at many things.

One of the girls had a good-sized pocketbook and the other a sweatshirt with a pouch. They both were looking around and acting suspicious.

The two girls must have felt comfortable as they started taking items and putting them in the pocketbook. Into the pocketbook went two of each item they coveted, presumably one for each girl. The only variation occurred when they chose shampoo and conditioner; they must have had their own preferences when it came to their hair. The girl with the sweatshirt put four items in her pouch as well.

After about ten minutes, the girls seemed to be satisfied with their choices and headed for the exit. I will say, it was entertaining to watch these two girls act all grown up while shoplifting, with no intention to pay.

The two made it only so far as the vestibule. They were detained and brought to the office. The female service manager was already in the office when the girls came up the stairs.

They sat down in the office, and I asked them why they weren't in school. No response. They also would not say how they had gotten to the store. They were on the punkish side, and they acted cocky, like, "What do you think you're going to do about it."

When I was given the total dollar amount of what they stole—$157.76, which I considered to be excessive—I called the police and not their parents. I eyed them looking at each other when I made the call.

Officers arrived, assessed the girls, and looked at me as I was pointing to the pile of beauty aids they had stolen. There were some food items as well. I told the officer how much the items had totaled and said they were not responsive to me either.

The officer immediately asked the girls for their names, and their whole demeanor changed. They answered all the officer's questions. They told him they'd skipped school.

They were handcuffed and seated in the back seat of the police cruiser. I thought that was a good move; they would always remember this ride with handcuffs on. I hoped it would teach them a lesson.

The half dozen times I have called the police for shoplifters under eighteen, I always got a letter from the juvenile court department, asking me to appear at the suspect's hearing. I did go to court for these two girls.

The few times I appeared in court, I was there for hours and never had a role. I think I simply represented the face of the victim, a reminder for the perpetrators as to what they had done wrong. That's what happened in this case as well.

I never learned the girls' situation. Their shopping list: two Venus razors, two Venus cartridges, two Nutrisse hair products, two feminine hygiene products, a Dove shampoo and conditioner, one each of Herbal Essence shampoo and conditioner, two cans of Edge shave gel for sensitive skin, two containers of Johnson and Johnson body talc, and enough candy and gum for a week.

Chapter 33
Lobster Delivery

Lobsters are one of the most shoplifted items, which might seem surprising given their size, shape, and the fact that they are alive. How could you put them in say, a pocketbook, diaper bag, or baby stroller?

Shoplifters found the ways.

Some walked straight out the door with them. Some got two bags of lobsters in the seafood department and later combined the bags, paying only the amount on the exterior bag. Still others concealed them under the shopping cart. Some, like our truck-driving long-hauler from the Midwest, put lobsters in a cooler.

This individual drove a tractor trailer for a well-known delivery company. His route took him back and forth from the Midwest to New England, where he would buy lobsters in our store, pack them in a cooler, and take them home. We thought he was buying them.

One day in 1997, though, the driver came in with a cooler, went to the seafood department, and ordered about forty lobsters. The clerk at the seafood counter noticed the man only put some of the bags of lobsters in the cooler; he put several other bags into his carriage.

Thinking this was odd behavior, the seafood clerk tried to call me to alert me, but by the time we communicated, the driver had already checked out and left.

After checking the surveillance camera footage and the register receipts, sure enough, the truck driver had only paid for the two bags of lobsters in his carriage—not the bags he had in his cooler. The cashier or bagger should have asked to look in the cooler, but she was intimidated by the size of the shoplifter, who stood six feet five inches and was built like he played middle linebacker. I might have had trouble asking if he had anything in his cooler as well.

I wondered if the driver forgot to pull the lobsters out of the cooler or if he purposely tried to deceive the check-out clerk. He'd purchased a few other things: a couple bags of ice and some Gatorade. I got a good photograph of him, showed the other managers, and put it in my file. I hoped we'd catch him next time.

And there was a next time.

About a month later, the truck driver came in with a cooler. I recognized the physique and grabbed the picture of him from the file, which also had attached the receipts from his prior visit and a list of what went unpaid.

Following the pattern, the tractor trailer guy put some bags of lobsters in his cooler and some in his carriage. I stopped him before he went through the registers. I showed him the photograph and the previous receipt, pointed at the cameras, and waited for his response. It was a little unsettling. He was a big dude.

"I truly forgot," he said, offering to pay what he owed us from the last shopping visit.

I didn't believe him but was grateful he wanted to pay. He agreed to come to the office. He was chatty once we were seated in the office. He told me about his route and how everyone back home loved lobster. He said he bought them in our store and resold them at home. He told me about his wife and kids and how long he'd been driving tractor trailers. I think he was nervous, and his guilty conscience was apparent.

He paid his debt.

"In the future," I told him, "put your lobsters in the cooler after you pay for them."

We shook hands, and he went down and checked out, paying for all of that day's lobsters.

This driver continued to come in about once a month to stock up, and pay for lobsters before heading to the Midwest.

Chapter 34
Organized Crime Rings

Wikipedia defines organized retail crime, or ORC, as "professional shoplifting, cargo theft, retail crime rings and other organized crime occurring in retail environments." Further, the website says that when one person acts alone, that is not considered ORC.

Organized criminals work in teams—with some members creating a distraction and others acting out the theft. They move from store to store and from city to city, stocking up on specified items as directed by a group leader. They steal meat, baby formula, razor blades, and whatever products the group can resell quickly for cash, through many means.

In my career, I learned that, yes, organized crime rings target supermarkets. I am sure any one of the stores I managed was a victim more times than I knew. There were many shoplifting incidents with two or more persons who were caught. Could have been ORC.

These crime rings sell items at pawn shops and flea markets, but the return is not as high, about thirty percent of value according to the United States Government Accountability Office. Another way to sell stolen goods is online—in a process called e-fencing—on sites like eBay, craigslist, Amazon, etc., and usually, there's a return of roughly seventy percent because these online shoppers are looking for a deal. Organized retail crime rings will often try to return stolen items back to the stores they robbed in exchange for cash or gift cards, which nets them the largest rate of return—one hundred percent.

One day in 2018, I was called by a supervisor, who told me to expect a call from an FBI agent from a neighboring state regarding an organized crime ring. The specific crime was credit card fraud, not shoplifting. The group had used stolen card numbers and illegally purchased cartons of Newport cigarettes in the store I was managing. Ring members also bought air conditioners and a carriage of groceries with the fraudulent cards. Three fraudulent cards were used in total.

One male member of the ring purchased the Newport cigarettes at the service center—eight cartons worth. The other male purchased the air conditioners at the checkout, and the females, a carriage of groceries. They were in the store less than fifteen minutes.

I explained all this to the agent when he contacted me. He had photographs and video from our loss prevention team and was gathering further evidence about this crime ring. Because this group was stealing in multiple states, the FBI was involved.

This was the first time I had talked to an FBI agent on a professional level.

He shared with me that the ringleader, who'd visited our store, had a wall of Newport cigarettes in his house—hundreds of cartons, from stores across the region. Every carton of our cigarettes was stamped with appropriate store number and address, that's how we were contacted. The cigarettes were obtained with phony credit cards, shoplifted, or stolen.

"The guy's girlfriend is spilling the beans on him—a scorned woman perhaps," the agent told me. It was a short conversation. That ring, consisting of the leader and multiple players, is still under investigation.

Many states, including Massachusetts, are changing their laws to combat organized retail crime. The law in Massachusetts is far from perfect, but it gives police and prosecuting attorneys a little more power to make arrests and prosecute these crime rings.

Chapter 35
Shoplifting on Steroids: Smash-and-Grab Mobs

Smash-and-grab mobs are similar to the likes of a flash mob, except for the outcome. Flash mobs organize, assemble quickly in a public place, perform or entertain, then disperse as fast as they came. Smash-and-grab mobs organize through a leader, appear at a retail store, smash windows and or display cases, grab merchandise from their shopping list, then run away without paying.

Shoplifting in bulk.

The phenomenon of smash-and-grab was common in the 1930s and '40s. Thieves would use bricks, hammers, and even stones to smash windows and reach in and grab the merchandise. This was done without the concern of setting off alarms or making noise. Merchants had to strengthen windows and display cases with stronger glass and even fit windows with protective bars. This helped prevent future incidents—until recently.

Eyewitness News ABC 7 in Los Angeles, California, reported on Friday December 3,2021, that with a recent run of large-scale, smash–and–grab robberies across the state, prosecutors and retailers were pushing back on California's governor and attorney general, claiming law enforcement officials have enough tools to combat the surge in retail theft, even though they didn't—and still don't. This is a direct result of a voter-approved easing of related laws, proposition 47, which passed in November 2014.

Prop 47 made shoplifting items worth a total of nine hundred and fifty dollars in value or less a misdemeanor, always. Previously, shoplifting could be charged as a burglary, a felony offense. The objective of Prop 47 was to focus on rehabilitation and not incarceration. It appears to not have worked as planned.

The Public Policy Institute of California reported in 2018 that Prop 47 led to a nine percent rise in larceny theft as compared to the 2014 larceny rate. Some large retailers reported a fifteen percent increase in shoplifting since the passage of Prop 47. Many think that number is even higher, as many thefts go unreported. The passing of Prop 47 led to low-risk, high-reward shoplifting.

Eyewitness News reported that Vern Pierson, immediate past president of the California District Attorneys Association and the district attorney in El Dorado County, said, "We cannot function as a society where we have told people over and over again that there is no consequence for stealing other people's property."

California Retailers Association president and CEO Rachel Michelin was quoted as saying, "We feel a little bit like we're under assault." Further, she said, shoplifting has been a rising problem, but recent large-scale, smash-and-grab thefts are "raising it to a whole new level."

Retail groups estimate the losses to be in the tens of billions of dollars nationally.

The rash of high-level theft even threatened public safety, as bands of criminals invaded stores full of innocent shoppers. Detective Jamie McBride of the Los Angeles Police Protective League told CBSN Los Angeles on December 14, 2021, that if you're thinking of coming to Los Angeles, California—don't. "We cannot protect you," McBride said, adding, "We can't guarantee your safety. It's really, really out of control."

Detective McBride said the pillaging reminded him of the movie "Purge," except, instead of having twenty-four hours to commit a crime, perpetrators instead had 365 days to commit whatever offenses they want.

Luxury stores in Los Angeles and Union Square in San Francisco were being terrorized by large mobs, swarming aisles and escaping with merchandise, as were high-end retailers such as Nordstrom, Louis Vuitton, and others across the country. Smash-and-grabs remain most notable in states with relaxed laws.

Thieves are recruited by organized retail crime rings. They are given a shopping list and are paid in cash for the merchandise they steal. Brick-and-mortar stores already battling online sales for a piece of the pie are outraged when these stolen goods end up for sale online at reduced prices. Whether it is on eBay, Amazon, Etsy, etc., the stolen goods are easily e-fenced in these online marketplaces, with deals too amazing to pass up

However, all this could change as journalists around the country are calling attention to the problem.

The Washington Post ran a story on December 10, 2021, written by Aaron Greg titled, "Retail CEOs say online marketplaces are fueling 'flash mob' robberies," in which Greg outlines the problem faced by big-box CEOs. Greg also reported that twenty CEOs from stores such as BestBuy, Home Depot, Target and seventeen other stores all signed a letter they sent to House and Senate leaders, asking for passage of the Inform Consumers Act. This act was designed to increase visibility around online, third-party sellers and unify retailers, merchants, manufacturers, and law enforcement in halting the sale of stolen and counterfeit goods sold online.

"Criminals are capitalizing on the anonymity of the Internet and failure of certain marketplaces to verify their sellers," Greg said the CEOs wrote in their letter.

The first version of the Inform Consumers Act bill was not voted on in 2021. The bill will come up for discussion in the 2022 session of Congress.

Changing laws to lessen penalties for stealing someone else's property only promotes low-risk, high-reward shoplifting. You can go before a judge and ask for leniency, but you can't ask for a tougher sentence when it is not the law.

Chapter 36
Meeting the Mayor

In 2011, working in a new store and learning the protocols of yet another police department, I pulled the mayor into a shoplifting conversation—because I could.

The matter was a shoplifter who had gotten out of the store with a carriage of meat on three separate occasions. We caught him after he left a carriage of meat behind in one of his attempts; we figured he thought he was being watched and aborted his plan, yet in doing so, he actually alerted us.

With a little detective work on the surveillance system, we found him walking out with carriages of meats in two prior incidents, both on weekend days in the early afternoon.

While we had surveillance photos of the suspect and were familiar with his appearance, we did not know his identity; we didn't know what kind of vehicle he drove or his plate number. What we knew was that his style was to hover around the express checkout, and when he thought no one was watching, he headed to the exit and out.

One weekend, we were ready for this guy. We took care not to alert him that we were watching him; we didn't want him to get paranoid and leave a full carriage a second time.

We knew that the grand total for his three shoplifting incidents was roughly one thousand dollars. We guessed based on the number of packages we could see in each of the carriages in the surveillance footage. Because I was new to the store, I was not yet familiar with the police officers or their procedures and approach to shoplifting. Perhaps I should have alerted them when we knew we had a suspect, but I chose not to as I wanted to catch him.

One Sunday afternoon, our meat shoplifter came in about one. He grabbed a carriage and went directly to the meat department at the back of the store, taking his time in gathering about thirty packages of meat, which he placed in his carriage. Then he headed up front.

There was one manager outside on the sidewalk with a portable phone. The front-end manager, also on alert, focused his attention away from the shoplifter, so as not to spook him. I waited, out of sight, by the service center. I had my portable phone with me. The suspect headed toward the door.

We caught up with him in the vestibule, and after a brief struggle, the shoplifter knew he was caught. We got him inside, and the police were called and on their way.

When the officer arrived, I related all the details, including that this man had shoplifted from us on three previous occasions. The officer arrested the shoplifter and took the information and photographs from the previous incidents. I told the officer we were looking for one thousand in restitution.

On the day the police were present, the dollar amount in meat taken was $345.23. The incident made the papers, and it became known that the shoplifter had multiple warrants out for his arrest—mostly bench warrants for various thefts and not appearing in court. He was headed to prison. The paper did not mention the prior shoplifting incidents. I called the officer to ask why.

"There was nothing more I can do because the case had already been tried in court," he said.

That didn't sit right with me. So, I called the mayor.

To give full disclosure, the mayor's brother worked full time at the store I managed, so I had an in. I also felt more comfortable discussing the issue with the mayor than the police chief at that point.

The mayor and I talked on the phone, and I told him about the shoplifting incident and that I objected that my store was not receiving the full restitution for the three thefts.

"I have no jurisdiction with the courts, but I might be able to help you get this situation settled," he told me.

He set up a meeting and invited the chief of police and his lieutenant to join us. We were all introduced.

It had been a few months since the shoplifter had been caught, arrested, and tried in court. When I brought up the matter of restitution, the police chief indicated that the lieutenant, as the liaison to the court, should answer.

"You need to write the district attorney a letter with how much restitution the store is looking for and why," the lieutenant told me, adding, "You are the victim of a crime." The lieutenant was familiar with the shoplifter and said, "He is back in prison, and there is not any restitution to get anyway." It was too late to write a letter for this incident as the judge had already ruled.

In the previous city where I was a store manager, the police would bring restitution information to the court. It was a large city, with fewer retail shopping outlets. It was a different district court as well. In this city, I would tell the arresting officer we were looking for restitution for an amount, give him all the facts and videos, and the officer would bring that information to court.

I had called the mayor because it was apparent his police department handled incidents slightly different. "When an officer comes to your store, he is there to make an arrest and not act as a negotiator," the police chief also explained when we met. This is a statement I had heard before.

The mayor listened to our conversation respectfully for about twenty-five minutes. At the conclusion, he asked me, "Are you all set?"

"Yes," I said.

It was comfortable and professional. I thought it was a productive meeting, and I was grateful to learn a few things about dealing with this particular police department. The air was clear on how things should happen moving forward.

Having a good relationship with the police became important in that store; there were more shoplifting incidents there per year than in any other store I had worked in before or since.

Chapter 37
Front Page of the College Newspaper

When I first became a store manager in 1993, there was a college in the neighboring town. In my first three and a half years at that store, one third of the shoplifters we caught—far too many at about seventy—were students at the college.

The young people were stealing cigarettes, mostly in cartons or packs. Cigarettes were still on the sales floor in the eighties, not under lock and key as they are today. Students also stole health and beauty items, pain relievers, toothpaste, pregnancy test kits, groceries, deli meats, and candy. More than half opted to pay civil recovery and not get the police involved. Perhaps so their parents would not find out.

Over time, I became acquainted with a professor from the college who also shopped at the supermarket. He always went out of his way to say hi to me when he came in. It crossed my mind on a number of occasions to talk to him about what was going on with all this shoplifting from the students. I finally asked him if he minded coming to the office so I could talk to him about this issue.

As I spoke about these shoplifting incidents, the professor was clearly shocked. He had no idea students were stealing from the store—and getting caught in such large numbers. I didn't talk to him about specific individuals. I generalized, telling him, for instance, that I thought maybe some students stole on a dare, or maybe as part of a frat house pledge. The professor promised to talk to a dean about the problem and get back to me.

Soon after, the dean of students did call me and suggested he send a staff member from the school newspaper—a student—to interview me. I thought it couldn't hurt and agreed. I got the call from a young lady who wrote for the paper, and we set up a time to meet and discuss the shoplifting problem happening at her college.

The student reporter showed up with a friend, and we talked in my office. The writer had done her homework and knew the laws and consequences of shoplifting in the state. We talked about how a record might blemish graduate school enrollment and possibly future job opportunities. We talked about civil recovery, as most of the college shoplifters opted for this instead of being arrested.

The amount of civil recovery was equal to the average cost of a college textbook at the time. The reporter asked about our procedures, and we discussed them. I explained that, as long as the student was cooperative, he or she could pay civil recovery and not be arrested. Shoplifting cost everyone time and money.

When the interview was done, the student promised to bring me the next edition of the newspaper when it was printed. She also staged a photograph of her friend putting a carton of cigarettes under his jacket. That photo appeared on the paper's front page with the story.

The student delivered a paper, as promised, and the publicity worked.

Over the next two years, there were only three incidents in which college students were caught shoplifting. I thought this was amazing. Maybe the students realized we were watching. Who doesn't read the college newspaper? I thanked the professor for his intervention the next time I saw him in the store.

There was only one problem with the front-page news: That issue of the student newspaper came out just before parents' weekend at the college. Not good PR. The president of the college had papers pulled from sight.

I remember college visits with my two kids. I wouldn't have wanted to see that front page either.

Chapter 38
Carriage Full of Tide Detergent

In 2012 and 2013, Tide laundry detergent made national headlines as it, too, had become a favorite item for organized retail crime rings to shoplift. It was easy to steal by loading up a carriage, covering it with something larger, and walking out the front door. The person who stole Tide, retailing over twenty dollars a bottle, could trade for five dollars cash, or ten dollars' worth of weed or crack cocaine, according to *New York Magazine*.

Tide is the United States' most popular laundry detergent. It is more expensive than most of its competitors. Apparently, Tide has some brand loyalty amongst thieves. Everybody uses laundry detergent, and it doesn't spoil.

The first time I witnessed a Tide theft, I had to ask myself, "Did I just see that happen?"

In fact, I did.

I was at the front end of the store with the front-end manager when I was paged to the service center and headed that way. I had only taken a few steps when I saw a heavy female with a long coat, wearing large sunglasses, pushing a carriage towards the exit. She had not gone through a cash register.

The carriage held two oversized bags of dog food, visible on the top. The product underneath did not appear to be bagged. After hesitating a second, I decided to head outside the store to ask this female if she had a receipt for her purchase. I caught up to her as she was walking down an aisle in the parking lot, well past the fire lane.

"Do you have a paid receipt for those items?" I asked her.

At that time, I noticed a couple dozen family-sized bottles of Tide laundry detergent underneath the dog food. No way she paid for that. I stopped the carriage, and she looked at me.

"Do you have a receipt for these items," I asked her again. She started digging in her purse.

This happened so quickly, there was no one to help me. As she searched futilely in her purse for a receipt I was sure she did not have, I gave the carriage a tug to indicate we were headed back inside. She tugged back, but she kept looking.

"I think I left the receipt in the van," she said.

"In your van?" I thought. She had only just exited the store.

She let go of the carriage and walked toward a white van about sixty feet away from where we stood. I pulled the carriage after her, but she climbed in the van and took off. I recorded her license plate number and used my portable phone to call my office manager, who called the police.

I was with the carriage still in the middle of the parking lot, making my way back to the store, when the police cruiser pulled up next to me. "Laundry detergent?" the officer asked incredulously.

"Yes," I said. "It's a first for me too." I gave the officer the suspect's plate number and let him know she was in a white van, headed for the highway. He said he would get back to me and quickly left.

There were twenty-three bottles of Tide detergent in the woman's carriage, retailing at $19.99 a bottle. Including the two bags of dog food, the total amount she'd attempted to get away with was $489.75, plus tax.

The officer came back, but alone. He had no luck finding the suspect. The plate number I gave him was wrong. (I guess I needed glasses.) I provided the officer with a photograph of the woman leaving the store. He said he would post it at the police station and on its webpage, in case another officer recognized her.

A few days later, a different police officer came to the store with a mugshot of the female, asking me if she was the same shopper who'd walked out of the store with the carriage of Tide. He said the woman in his photo had an opioid addiction.

"Yes, it could be," I told him. It was hard to judge as, in my surveillance photo, she had sunglasses on, but I was ninety-nine percent sure it was her.

The good news was she did not get away with the carriage full of Tide, but the bad news was we had yet another department to keep an eye on for shoplifting activity.

I wondered if we would have to put Tide detergent under lock and key.

We couldn't lock up the whole store.

Chapter 39
The Crying Shoplifter

A few shoplifters cried when they were caught. Many put on an act, begging for forgiveness. One person I recall became a blubbering, crying, snot-coming-down-his-nose shoplifter. From the moment we asked him if he forgot to pay for the items in his backpack, and until he was escorted to the police cruiser, he was distraught.

He came into the supermarket with a pack on his back. He did his best to be incognito, but he didn't do a very good job. We had eyes on him as he was acting suspiciously, nervously glancing around, not making eye contact. A number of associates pointed this suspect out. Plus, he had a pack on his back.

A young person—about twenty, slight build—he wore glasses. The first thing I saw him steal was a package of Poly-Grip adhesive for dentures. He took his pack off in the health and beauty aids aisle and put the Poly-Grip in the pack.

He continued through the aisles, adding groceries in his carrier as well. He did not even try to pretend to go through the registers. He simply headed for the door.

My associate manager stopped him in the vestibule and escorted him to the office. When he sat down, he was already crying. The value of the items he'd shoplifted was $37.99.

The shoplifter sobbed so uncontrollably he could not even answer questions. The police were called. I guessed our latest suspect was either under the influence of drugs or was a total emotional wreck. He wept through what seemed like a roll of paper towels before the police came on the scene.

When the police officer asked the shoplifter for his identification, the young man began a new level of breakdown. The officer eventually cuffed him and took him to the cruiser for a ride to the police station.

This was a quantum-level shoplifting experience for me. Total sobbing. Not within my expertise to evaluate.

I was glad the local police could step in and hopefully find an appropriate mentor or program to offer the kid some help.

Chapter 40
When Employees Steal

I prided myself on hiring honest, dedicated people.

Young people, still in school, typically didn't have a resume or any previous work experience, so I always asked to see a report card. I wasn't so much interested in the grades but in what the teachers had to say about the student. I looked for "a pleasure to have in class" and shied away from "disruptive in class."

Sadly, some schools have done away with teacher comments, probably to avoid liability. But back then, the feedback was telling. If a student had unflattering comments, I would ask them to come back the next grading cycle, and if the comments had improved, I would hire them. This happened often.

With adults, I relied some on my intuition, sizing them up. Would they be a good fit with others in the supermarket? I steered away from individuals who'd had four jobs in the last year. Red flag. It was an investment of time and money to train an employee, so someone who was apt to be around only for a short time wasn't worth the effort.

As careful as I was in hiring, I still managed to hire some bad seeds. I think that's an inevitable part of the hiring process.

When student workers stole from the store, I usually called the parents. If the theft carried a high-dollar price tag, or the kid was a punk, I would call the police. Stealing from your employer was not considered shoplifting, but larceny.

Some examples of employee theft included eating items without paying for them or giving discounts to friends or coworkers at the register by passing an item over the scanner in such a way it doesn't ring up; this is called "sliding," and it is not easy to catch. Some of the sliding incidents I have been involved with racked up into hundreds of dollars.

One busy shopping day in 2012, I was walking the front main aisle and saw a male customer walking towards me, looking at each cashier. He found who he was looking for and yelled to his wife to come his way. This was odd, as he bypassed open registers to get in a line in which he'd have to wait.

When the customers in question put their groceries on the register belt, I was already in the office, watching. The cashier, who was definitely an accomplice, scanned two packages at the same time. Only the one on top rang up, but the higher-priced package underneath did not. This was 'sliding.' She repeated the process quite a few times—a little less than a hundred dollars' worth in theft.

By using this motion, unless you watched closely, you could not tell anything was amiss. The packages were set up by the couple in line. They used the plastic bags the store offered for items such as meat, which can ooze. The couple put two items in one plastic bag, with the lower-priced item on the top. The three of them had done this before.

The cashier had only recently moved to the area, transferring from a store in the town she previously lived in. Thankfully, she had not been at the store I was managing for long. I confronted this group and brought them all to the office. We settled with civil recovery for the amount of five hundred dollars. The cashier was fired. Building a case for previous incidents would have been very time consuming.

Another way employees can steal is by manually entering the cost for an item, rather than scanning the barcodes. Nothing should have been rung up manually. This type of crime happened multiple times, on three orders, all at the end of a night shift.

Reviewing video from the previous evening, we'd watch a cashier manually ring in a higher-priced item for a dime. We called that a "sweetheart deal." We could also catch this form of theft the day after in reviewing and assessing transactions with the assistance of computer software that does analysis.

In one year, we found three employees were giving multiple sweetheart deals. Their parents were called, and they all lost their jobs. The loss we incurred wasn't substantial, and I don't think they had stolen on multiple occasions, but they were setting a bad example. They were good kids and made a mistake, but they couldn't work at the store anymore. We ran a business, not a high school, and hopefully everyone learned and moved on.

At the end of each evening, as part of closing procedures, cashiers and baggers put overstock away, and this presented yet another opportunity for staff to shoplift. Items that customers didn't want were to be restocked on the shelves.

One evening, a cashier putting overstock away decided to do some shopping too. She put some of the food away and kept a few bags she'd put her "shopping" in, yet there were no registers open, given the hour.

The supermarket makes an announcement at the end of the day that the store is closing, and final purchases must be made. Employees are also given an opportunity to make a purchase before the store closes.

This cashier didn't purchase her items but left her carriage at the spot where employee final purchases are kept. A register receipt is supposed to be attached to this final purchase. This cashier never had a receipt. Unfortunately for her, a manager did his job and asked to see a receipt. The cashier, her mom, and I agreed on a restitution amount that would be paid. The cashier couldn't work at the store anymore.

Some of the young people who stole from us thought they were clever, but it didn't turn out that way.

We built a lot of vendor displays years ago to promote contests we were holding in regard to particular products. One football season, we hung a blanket with a football theme over a beer display.

A few weeks later, the blanket went missing. This was before security cameras, so we investigated by talking to people and honed in on a young man who worked in the grocery department, although he denied stealing the blanket. He quit a couple weeks later.

We reported the theft, and an officer came and recorded our suspicions. We also gave him a photo of the blanket.

Months passed, and there was a drug bust at an apartment in the next town. What was hanging on the wall of the apartment? The blanket. Who lived in the apartment? The grocery clerk who worked the Saturday night that the blanket disappeared.

The officer returned the blanket to the store. In addition to facing drug charges, the grocery clerk was also charged with possession of stolen merchandise.

Some young thieves also stole beer. One Saturday morning in the early 1990s, we'd just opened the door for another day of business. A few minutes later, a police officer came strolling through the vestibule with a Cheshire cat smirk on his face. He held two cases of beer.

"Guess where I found these?" he said to me, smiling. I was completely baffled.

"Don't know," I responded. "Where?"

The officer said he'd been making his rounds on the overnight shift and pulled in to patrol the parking lot, which was dark, as the store had been closed for a couple of hours. The lot lights were off, yet he saw a light from a car in the middle of the lot.

The officer approached the vehicle and spotted a young man in the parking lot, lifting the lid off a fifty-five-gallon trash barrel. The young man was guilty of something, according to the officer.

The policeman used his flashlight and looked around and inside the barrel. Underneath the trash bag were the two cases of beer. Upon questioning, the young man—a store employee—admitted he put the cases there during the closing shift he'd worked that evening.

There were no surveillance cameras in the store or in the parking lot. As a bagger, the young man's duties were gathering carriages in the parking lot and bagging groceries at the checkout, and he was also frequently assigned to gather the barrels of trash in the parking lot at the end of the night.

The officer learned the young man had put the barrel on a dolly and rolled it into the store's backroom. He removed the trash, threw it in the compactor, and when no one was around, he grabbed two cases of beer from the beverage area of the backroom, and placed them in the bottom of the barrel and covered them with a thrash bag. He took the barrel back out to the parking lot to retrieve later.

This maneuver could not happen every night as there were ten to fifteen baggers working at any given time. It was never certain who would get the task of throwing away the trash from the parking lot.

Who knows how long this theft would have carried on if the officer hadn't accidentally made the catch? How long it had been going on?

The young man's punishment was out of my hands. He was a minor, caught, and arrested.

A riskier theft took place under my watch in the late eighties, when Kodak 35-milimeter film was at the height of its popularity, arguably the best-selling film worldwide. As young people have cellphones with cameras today, back then they had cameras, into which you loaded film. It was kept on display in multiple locations, and it wasn't cheap at about $6.99 a roll.

I usually spent most of my nights on duty watching the checkout areas. Every fifteen minutes or so, I'd make the rounds of other departments, gathering overstock and making sure the back room was clean and neat. I would then head back to the checkout, where all customers came and went, and I'd repeat my rotation of these steps until the store closed.

Early on in my career, a senior manager taught me to change up my routine every now and then. I did so this night.

I had just finished walking the meat aisle and went through the now-dark meat room to the back room. I would normally have continued to inspect the produce department. As I passed through the door, a young clerk was standing next to the cardboard compactor. He looked frightened and immediately walked away. I didn't think much about it until I heard some noise as I approached the compactor.

In the compactor, was another employee—a bagger—holding a box that had contained seventy-two packages of Kodak film. One by one, the bagger was pushing rolls of film through a gap in the container; they fell to the ground, where he planned to retrieve them later. This was dangerous, as the compactor crushes cardboard for easy transport; when full, the containers are replaced with an empty container.

The lookout was standing guard to protect the bagger from being crushed or killed. I assume he would have prevented someone from pushing the button to the compactor.

I asked the young man to climb out of the compactor and bring all the film he had left in the box. I took the film from his possession, and we headed to the office. As we walked, he told me he sold the film at the high school he attended.

"I will need to call your parents," I told him. He pleaded with me, but my mind was made up. When we got near the office, though, he ran out the door to employee parking, got in his car, and drove off.

This was a pretty stupid move, as I knew who he was. I called the police. The officer arrived quickly, and I explained the situation. We went around the back of the building to collect the large pile of film on the ground next to the compactor. The officer took all the information and left.

The next day, I got a call from the bagger's mother. She had said the police had visited their house, and her son had admitted to the theft. She thanked me for giving him an opportunity to work at the store.

I didn't ask the bagger's mother or the officer what punishment was meted out, but I was pleased the mother had called.

I decided the school principal should also know what was happening under his watch. I called and left a message with his secretary. He called me back about an hour later. The conversation didn't go so well.

"How do you know what happens at this school?" he asked me. "I assure you that stolen film is not being sold here. That is not happening here!"

These types of theft happen more than I would like. It's tough telling a good employee that they can't work at the supermarket anymore because of a mistake in judgement.

When managers steal, the value is usually substantial, and the police are called. Loss prevention, the division of the supermarket chain that investigates theft, gets involved. As a store manager my only involvement would be as a witness. I wasn't always privy to results of these investigations.

Chapter 41
Pregnant Shoplifter

This young female was cute as a button but had a real bad attitude. She appeared to be shopping with an older woman. She was seen by the front-end manager in the health and beauty aids aisle, acting suspiciously. The suspect had two bottles of supplements in her hand. She had been looking around nervously, and would go away from, and then come back to, the older woman's shopping cart. I can't say for certain if the older woman knew what was going on.

After the older woman left the aisle, the young female stayed in the aisle another couple minutes. She still had the supplements in her hand. As we watched on the cameras, the young female put them into the bag that was hanging over her shoulder. We had a shoplifter.

The young girl finally left the aisle and caught up with the older lady. We watched while the two continued shopping.

When it looked as if the two were done shopping and heading to the registers, the young female with the supplements left the carriage and headed to the door. She was stopped in the vestibule and brought to the office. I asked the girl to put the two bottles of supplements she had concealed onto my desk.

The attitude started.

"I haven't done anything!" she said. "Why am I here?"

I stopped listening and went back down to the registers to talk to the woman who had accompanied the young girl in the store. When this woman finished paying for the groceries, I approached her. I let her know we had her companion in my office and that she had been caught shoplifting.

The woman told me that was her granddaughter. The grandmother came to the office with me. The two bottles of supplements were still not on my desk. I told the grandmother there were two bottles of supplements in her granddaughter's bag.

The grandmother told the girl to take them out of her purse. There was one bottle of prenatal vitamins, and the other bottle was melatonin, a sleep aid. Total was $26.89. There was a little talking between the two, and the grandmother up and left.

I asked where she was going. She said, "Home," and that I should call the girl's grandfather. Normally, I would have let the girl go, but it was plain grandma wanted nothing to do with her.

The shoplifter had an attitude, and maybe lied to me twice. The supplements were for her sister, and then they were for her friend. Grandma didn't buy the stories, so I guessed I shouldn't either.

The shoplifter was under eighteen. She offered to call her grandfather, but I called the police instead. This young girl needed to be taught a lesson. The officer came and arrested her. The grandfather arrived about a half hour later, but his granddaughter had already been arrested; she was gone, and that did not please him.

I was summoned to juvenile court for this case, but I did not appear. I thought it would be a waste of my time for this shoplifter. By appearing in juvenile court, I was the face of the victim. Minor shoplifters were usually put on probation, which she was.

Chapter 42
Receipt in Hand, Carriage Full of Groceries

Reusable bags were introduced in Australia during the nineties and caught on in the United States in 2000. The problem they presented to merchants was more and more consumers began to shop with them, rather than using a basket or carriage. We had to keep an eye out for the shoppers who didn't go through the register after packing them.

In a parallel strange phenomenon, it seemed that customers who packed their own groceries in these bags with the intent to leave without paying for them always had a receipt in hand. They waved the receipt proudly, like a flag, to show employees that their groceries were paid for. It's as if they thought by having the receipt visible, they had a ticket out of the supermarket.

This incident happened in May 2018. I spotted a middle-aged female in the soda aisle with a carriage full of groceries all neatly packed in reusable bags. I stopped at the end of the aisle and hid out of sight to see what she was doing.

There was no time to get to the surveillance cameras.

She put three cases of Monster Energy drinks under her carriage. Did she plan to come back to get the drinks after she checked out?

This female then went to her pocketbook and pulled a receipt out. Maybe she had paid for her packed groceries? She was headed my way, and I moved to another aisle. She was in the front main aisle of the store, heading to the service center and express registers.

Her back was to me, and I stayed close enough to make sure she paid for the energy drinks. I was sure she did not have those on her receipt. If she had told me she had paid for them, I planned to ask her for her receipt, to make sure. This was not normal, the way she was shopping. Normally, shoppers left their carriage with the groceries they'd paid for at the checkout and went back for what they'd forgotten.

She was past the express registers, and I thought she was going to the service center. The female went by the service center and stopped at the ATM. The ATM was not past the point of sale, and I went to an open express register to watch her. She put the receipt in her mouth and pretended to use the ATM. She did not even have a card in her hand.

Twenty seconds later she was headed for the door. I yelled for the front-end manager and got his attention. We were both pursuing her and caught her in the fire lane. The female gave us the receipt and said she paid for everything in her carriage. Problem was, the front-end manager noticed the receipt was dated a month earlier. April.

My front-end manager got her turned around, and the three of us headed back to the store. All the while, the female kept insisting she'd paid for the carriage of groceries. She kept digging in her pocketbook trying to find the correct receipt.

She continued to look feverishly for it as we sat down in my office. The police were called, and the female service manager was in the office with us. The shoplifter kept insisting it was the right receipt.

When the police officer showed up, the female shoplifter's story changed one hundred and eighty degrees. She told the police officer that she did walk out without paying. The total amount of the carriage was $318.19, mostly in higher-priced meats. The three packages of Monster Energy drinks came to $45.

We had the woman no trespassed. This shoplifter was a regular customer, and I recognized her. No one can convince me it was her first time stealing from the store.

Chapter 43
The Judge and the Courtroom

I have been to court a few dozen times for a wide range of cases—
shoplifting mostly, but also for slips and falls in the supermarket and
lawsuits brought by customers who'd been hit by identified falling
objects (cans, boxes, bottles, etc.) in the market, who found foreign
objects in their food, or whose vehicles were damaged by shopping
carts. I have testified a couple dozen times in the two states in which
I worked, raising my right hand and swearing to tell the truth, so help
me God, and sitting down next to the judge.

Some courthouses were modest. Some were old, and some were
so elaborate they annoyed me, such as one superior court with four
floors, twenty-four courtrooms, ten-foot-high doors, and mahogany
from Jamaica in every courtroom. Seemed an excessive use of
taxpayer money to me.

Civilians, low-level criminals summoned to court, and witnesses
testifying in court, had to pass through security; they and their
belongings passed through a metal detector, and there were no cell
phones allowed. If you happened to bring your cell phone with you,
you were turned away.

Lawyers, police officers, and other officers of the court bypassed
security with a badge or a wave. They did not have to wait in line
and could have possession of their cell phones. The criminals who
were locked up and had a court appearance, came through the back,
handcuffed, with a police escort.

Passing through security one day, I forgot I had my cell phone with
me. I had to go back to my truck, parked blocks away, to drop it off. On
another occasion, same courthouse, I had a multi-tool in my wallet.
They took it and gave me a coupon to pick it up on my way out.

Once in a courtroom, I seated myself in the back and waited. The bailiff would announce, "All rise," and the judge would enter, the boss of the room, without question.

The bailiff instructed those present to be seated, but only after the judge entered and sat down on the bench, seated above all others—physically head and shoulders above everyone else, including the jury, if there was one.

The attorneys and their clients sat in front of the judge; the jury box and witness stand always to the judge's left.

All the shoplifting cases I was involved in were overseen by a judge, sans jury. As the judge listened to all the testimony, at some point I was called to talk about what I had witnessed in each shoplifting incident.

This scenario played out most often early in my career, before video cameras. The one-room courthouse back then was in the same town as the college. Any shoplifter I caught was going to go before the judge, and I had to be there.

I would show up at nine in the morning and meet with the chief of police, who acted as prosecuting attorney, to discuss the shoplifting case. A shoplifting event could have been months old by the time the court date arrived.

The judge would, one by one, call the cases for that day. He read the charges and asked each defendant how he or she wanted to plead. If the defendant pleaded guilty, the judge would assess a fine and/or another form of punishment and move to the next case. In the case of these guilty pleas, I was free to go. My presence was important, though, so the shoplifter would see me and know I was ready to testify.

If the defendant pleaded innocent, the case would be continued until after the judge got through the first round of cases for that day. In such cases, I would have to testify. I would be sworn in and tell the judge what I'd witnessed. Then the shoplifter would be sworn in and give his side of the story.

After hearing all the evidence, the judge made a determination. Larceny shoplifting cases were considered misdemeanors, and fines usually ranged between one and two hundred dollars; often, the shoplifter was also put on probation. The judge could also order special conditions, such as a stay-away—or a no trespass—order. The judge further had the option to dismiss the case for lack of evidence, although that did not happen in any of my shoplifting cases.

The court proceedings never took more than a day and usually finished up right after lunch. The first couple of times testifying was a little nerve wracking. The more I took the stand, the easier it became.

This was not the case on my last day in court before I retired. It was 2019.

The case was a slip-and-fall incident. I was in the elaborate superior courthouse with the ten-foot-high doors. It was a civil case, and the plaintiff was asking for a multi-million-dollar settlement. She was a professional, and as a result of her injuries from her alleged slip and fall, could not continue to do her work.

The attorney representing the supermarket advised me I would have to testify. This slip and fall happened in a previous store I managed and not the one I was currently in. This was not a shoplifter stealing a carton of cigarettes; there were millions of dollars on the line. I was very nervous.

This slip and fall allegedly happened roughly six years before the court date. Criminal cases take priority over civil cases, and this case finally had its day in court.

The attorney coached me. He told me to look at the jury and be deliberate with my words. I was there to testify as to the supermarket's protocols in inclement weather. The jury consisted of twelve persons.

One other interesting fact about this case was the plaintiff never reported the incident when it happened. The plaintiff alleged that she was walking in the supermarket and slipped on water in the entrance to the store. The plaintiff claimed a young employee helped her to her feet, and she continued shopping, never mentioning her fall to a manager.

Four months after the alleged fall, the plaintiff's attorney sent a registered letter to the supermarket. Video for this incident, if it had been recorded, would have been recorded over by that point, so there was no video documentation. The plaintiff also came into the store at a later time, during a different bad-weather day, and took pictures where her slip had allegedly taken place.

There were opening arguments, and then the plaintiff testified. The trial lasted two days, and I testified at the end of the first day.

My attorney asked me, "What happens at the supermarket when there is inclement weather"?

I answered, "It is like a fire drill." I said this clearly as I looked between the attorneys in front of me to the wall in the back of the courtroom. I was loud and clear, but I couldn't look at the jury. I was too nervous and focused on the wall.

I explained that rugs are put down on the floor, caution cones are put in place, and mop and buckets were used at all entrances and exits to soak up extra moisture. I said we constantly cleaned clean up snow or rain that was tracked into the store.

The law says we don't have to be perfect, but we must make an attempt to keep the areas safe.

The plaintiff's attorney then cross-examined me. He showed some of the pictures the plaintiff had taken. They were of small areas in and at the entrance of the store.

"Where is the cone, and where is the mop and bucket?" he asked me. I attempted to tell him that it was more than likely out of the view in the pictures.

"Do you see them anywhere in this picture," he interrupted. I didn't argue and told him they were not in the picture. He showed the picture to the jury.

This continued with two more photographs, both offering small views of the inside of the store. I answered likewise. He continued questioning me about our procedures, and I answered. It was a nerve-racking fifteen minutes. When there were no further questions, I stepped down.

It was a serious irony that, after the first day of testimony ended, the judge dismissed the jury, one row at a time, beginning with the first. The first juror in the second row caught his foot and fell down two steps. An ambulance arrived, and there was commotion for the next hour. A slip and fall, during a slip and fall trial.

The case proceeded the next day with only eleven jurors, after the judge and attorneys agreed it was acceptable.

Even though my part was done, our attorney said I should appear in the courtroom the second day to show concern for the outcome. Once the jury was dismissed to deliberate, I could leave.

I was back at the supermarket when I got the call. We'd won!

Chapter 44
I Got Jumped in the Supermarket

Some shoplifters had particular nerve. Like the nineteen-year-old male who was high when he came in to do some shoplifting on a warm May Day in 2019. He got a carriage and had a shopping list. I suspect he was opioid dependent, looking for items to sell or trade for his drugs. My assistant manager spotted this kid right away.

The shopper started gathering items, bobbing and weaving with his carriage. He went down the detergent aisle and loaded up on five bottles of Tide and one bottle of Formula 409 cleaner. Then, he headed to the meat department and put two fresh pork shoulders in his carriage. Lastly, he strolled down the paper aisle and topped off his carriage with a large twelve-pack of Quilted Northern toilet tissue. Value of his cart: $146.31.

Our shoplifter then headed for the door.

When he got there, several managers were there to greet him. The shoplifter tried to get away, running back into the store. My assistant grabbed him and took him down to the ground, with the help of a few other managers.

The shoplifter was stronger than the average person. It took a couple managers and a customer or two to hold him on the ground until the police arrived. There was a lot of damage from the aftermath of this struggle.

The police arrived quickly and handcuffed the shoplifter, who was not talking. I asked the officer to no trespass him, and they took our suspect to the station. I indicated to the officer that we would assess the damage and seek restitution.

The next day, about mid-morning, the same teen showed up at the store. He was at the service desk. The assistant service manager recognized him and called me.

"What does he want?" I asked her. He should have been told by the police to stay away.

She posed my question to the shoplifter, who responded, "I was jumped here yesterday I lost my car keys."

There was no mention of the crime he'd committed. The assistant service manager found his keys in Lost and Found and turned them over.

Selective memory is bliss.

Chapter 45
Communication: Be on the Lookout,
BOLO Reports

With advances in technology, the internet age, social media, and cameras everywhere, all shoplifters should eventually get caught.

These days, most police departments, DA offices, and even the FBI issue alerts on social media platforms from Facebook to Twitter to Instagram. They post photographs of suspects and ask for help. The supermarket I worked at also used these platforms to help catch shoplifters. I am old enough to remember most-wanted pictures at the local post office, before social media.

On occasions we would get BOLO alerts—Be on the Lookout— from our loss prevention team. These alerts would include pictures, names, makes and models of cars, license plate numbers, and what shoplifters had stolen in any one of our stores. The alert would also describe how the event happened. The shoplifters had gotten away, and loss prevention wanted all stores to keep an eye out for these would-be criminals. Before camera systems and video, this was almost impossible. Today, on many occasions, these alerts help catch or deter shoplifting incidents.

Some of these reports from our loss prevention division came from thefts from other chain stores' loss prevention teams. With the onslaught of organized crime rings, competitors in the marketplace began to team up and share information. Other reports came from state governments, police departments, and most wanted sites, relevant to supermarkets. All of this was to keep management informed and to share the information of crime rings and shoplifters working in our trading area.

I used some of these tools at work, in weekly staff meetings. I wanted my team to have information and know what to look for. Shoplifting was a topic in most of my meetings, especially around the holidays, where there is always an uptick in criminal activity.

In one such report, the BOLO alert came to the main office from a competitor. Loss prevention at my company passed it along to our stores.

The competing supermarket caught two suspects—a male and a female—shoplifting in one of their stores. When the police looked into the trunk of the suspect's car, they found shrimp and meats with price stickers from the store I managed. That was embarrassing.

I was asked by loss prevention to look at the surveillance videos from the night the crime occurred to see if I saw the suspects in the store. I took a good look but did not see them, day or night. Loss prevention wanted evidence so we could prosecute these two shoplifters. Our loss prevention team had the capability to do the research from the main office as well. I never found out if they were able to find them in my store.

The good news is the shoplifters were caught and arrested.

Chapter 46
Spotting a Shoplifter

Not all shoplifters are easy to spot. There are signs to look for, but in every case, we had to be sure.

On a hot July day, for instance, a customer wearing a puffy jacket or a sweatshirt could have been attempting to steal. But he or she could also have been cold. We'd keep an eye out.

A customer who came in the store and unfolded four or five sales flyers might have been attempting to hide merchandise under the paper. That person was worth watching.

Here's an overview of the signs and tells we looked for as we did surveillance:

• Persons under the influence, and they were usually easy to spot. Addicts were in the store to steal. Period. Whether they were high or needed a fix, they were there to steal to support their habit. They usually did not have the traditional shopping pattern; start in one aisle and finish in the last aisle. They would take a shopping cart or carry basket and head directly to the meat department or shrimp section to fill up, and then look for a way out. This happened rather quickly and usually ended in a struggle.

• Persons looking around nervously, in a non-focused way, not necessarily looking to find an item on a shelf. They'd look at employees. Watch where employees were and whether they were paying attention. These shoplifters rarely made eye contact. They were constantly looking at the security cameras. If the person had merchandise on them, they were looking for a vacant aisle to conceal the items on their person, or they might just walk out the front door.

• Shoppers wearing sunglasses were also a little suspicious. Yes, some people are sensitive to bright lights. Most, though, put sunglasses on top of their heads, or they tucked them away while shopping.

• Persons peeling price stickers off products. Were they putting a lower price on a higher-priced item?

• Persons exiting the building quickly, without going through the registers. Perhaps they were having an emergency—or they were shoplifting.

• Customers with baby carriages and diaper bags. All moms with babies are not shoplifters, but I always watched baby carriages and large diaper bags. Many of the shoplifters I caught used the baby carriage or diaper bag to conceal merchandise, especially diaper bags. There was even a female who had a life-like doll in her baby carriage, and she used it to steal groceries. Large diaper bags that were in the carriage, laid flat, with few contents, were a dead giveaway the bag would be filled up.

• Large pocketbooks, shoulder bags, backpacks, gym bags, etc. were always watched, for caution's sake. Over the shoulder bags were easy to open quickly with one hand, while items were dropped in it with the other. Open pocketbooks or shoulder bags in the baby seat of the carriage, with expensive items scattered on top or around were something to watch.

• Customers with baggy clothing were also watched. Multiple pockets could get filled.

• As Chapter 23 suggests, customers who hold a meeting or have a discussion before entering the supermarket earn surveillance. They could be criminals forming a plan, rather than neighbors, catching up.

• Customers returning an item for refund, approaching the service center from inside the store, instead of the parking lot—as in Chapter 9—are also a big red flag.

• Shoppers with a receipt in hand in the store are likely to attract attention. Usually, these folks are pretending they paid for the groceries in their carriage.

• Customers making a scene are also another tell-tale sign. While the front-end manager is helping someone who pretends to be sick or hurt, causing a distraction, a partner on the other end of the store could be walking out with a carriage of groceries. Distractions include fights, lost wallets, and all kinds of performances.

As I said, customers displaying these traits are not necessarily shoplifting, but they do raise notice, and they should be watched.

Chapter 47
Stealing Aluminum Foil

In the winter of 2011, in a city supermarket I managed adjacent to a large shopping mall, two females were spotted acting suspiciously in the candy aisle. They were looking around. One tucked multiple packages of candy into her pocketbook. The same female went to the next aisle, where aluminum foil was on the shelf, and she pocketed a package of that as well. It easily fit into her large bag. Then, the women headed for the exit.

We met them at the door. The suspect with the items in her possession did not want to go to the manager's office. There was a struggle, and a customer injured his hand trying to help us. The female with the candy and foil eventually relented, and her partner in crime—who we had no evidence against—was allowed to leave. The police were called, and we waited for them. The injured customer waited as well.

After he arrived, the officer assessed the situation: Less than fifteen dollars in value, but he was interested, nevertheless. He focused on the aluminum foil.

"What do you need this for?" he asked our shoplifter. He did not let her answer. Instead he said, "You're going to line your pocketbook with it and go to the mall to steal, aren't you?"

Any bag lined with foil is referred to as a "booster bag," because a shoplifter can conceal items in it and a leave any store without triggering anti-theft devices at the entrances and exits. Possession of a booster bag is against the law.

Our supermarket did not have security equipment at its exits in this store, but gates at stores in the mall were equipped with radio transmitters and receivers. Only a few layers of aluminum foil are needed in a bag to pass through the security gate with contraband undetected.

Our shoplifter, who was from another state and had a record of shoplifting, was stealing so she could keep stealing.

The officer arrested her. She was charged with shoplifting as well as assault, for harming our customer.

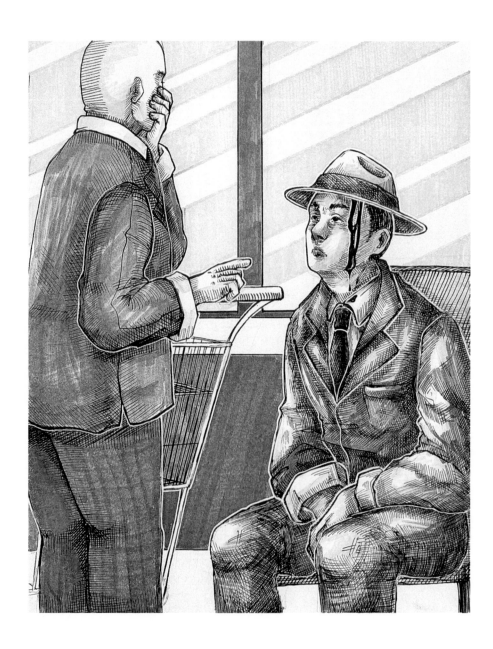

Chapter 48
Stories from Other Managers

These tales come from colleagues of mine who are also store managers. They illustrate that there is no shortage of shoplifting stories.

Bloody mess

In the late 1970s, this future manager was bagging groceries while his store manager chatted with some regular customers seated on benches in the front of the store.

While talking to one, the manager noticed blood was trickling down the side of the man's face. The customer was wearing a fedora hat, and the blood was slowly trickling down.

"Are you okay?" the manager asked.

The customer said yes and wiped the blood from his face. But it continued to trickle.

Concerned for the customer's health, the manager took the hat off the man's head to see where the blood was coming from. A package of steak was concealed under there. Its seal had broken, and the liquid inside—called purge—was the extent of his injury.

Ninja catwalker

In the era before surveillance cameras, about 1988, all surveillance was done on the catwalk. The manager of one city store required one associate to be on the catwalk for one hour each day as part of his daily shift, so there was always a lookout up there.

This associate, a future manager, saw a young man walking around with four packages of steak. The suspect was acting suspiciously, and the associate knew these steaks would never see a conveyor belt at the registers. He called the front-end manager from the catwalk phone, explained the situation, and gave the front-end manager a description of the suspect.

Moments later, the suspect put the steaks in his jacket.

After the associate hung up the phone, as he remembered it, he moved quickly to get out of the catwalk, which also held heating and ventilation air handlers, refrigeration lines on the ground, and sprinkler pipes in case of fire.

You had to duck from an air handler, so you didn't hit your head on it. You had to tight rope on refrigeration pipes, so you wouldn't trip on them. Trying to get out of the catwalk and down to the floor quickly could be the obstacle course in an "American Ninja Warrior" TV show.

With some effort, the associate got off the catwalk, down on the floor, and ran to the front to help. When he got there, he noticed the shoplifter was already outside, and the front-end manager was at the other entrance. The associate ran out of the store and got hold of the suspect. The front-end manager came to help.

"Thank God this happened in my younger days, and I could run," this manager told me.

Turning the tables

A manager and an associate approached a shoplifter around the year 2010 after the suspect was past the point of sale. The suspect had concealed steaks on his person and was heading toward the door. There was a struggle, but the manager and associate detained the shoplifter and brought him back into the store. The shoplifter was yelling, "Leave me alone."

To the shoplifter's rescue came a female customer, who told the manager to leave the suspect alone and then began recording a video of the action on her cell phone. The manager told her the man was suspected of stealing, but the female vigilante continued, "You have no right to do that. Let him go."

She carried on until the manager asked her, "What if he'd stolen your pocketbook?" He pointed to the customer's purse.

She hesitated, put her cell phone away, and left.

Shrimp tackle

Over thirty years ago, a manager I know watched a suspect moving through his store with two bags of shrimp, as he had a good idea that the shopper did not intend to pay. Problem was, the guy was six feet four inches and built. The manager had a couple high school football players bagging groceries that night and told them to be ready to help. The big guy headed for the door, making it through the first exit.

The manager was on him at the second door. Consider here that automatic doors open slowly for a reason—so people on either side have time to step out of the way and don't get struck. That also gave the manager time to catch the shoplifter. They both hit the outside door with so much force it came off the hinges; the pins on top and bottom just gave loose. The manager and shoplifter fell to the ground on top of the door, and the two football players were right there to help detain the suspect until police arrived. Somehow, no glass was broken.

Injured on the job

Sometimes, employees got hurt intervening in shoplifting cases, such as the time when a manager and meat clerk approached a customer who had exited without paying for an expensive box of shaved meat. The shoplifter told the manager his girlfriend was inside paying—a statement the manager knew to be false.

The manager asked the shoplifter to come back into the store. The three of them got the carriage turned around and headed back into the store. Then the shoplifter bolted, giving the manager a swift kick to the side of his knee as he passed. The manager crashed to the ground. The meat clerk gave chase but lost the shoplifter, who now also faced an assault charge.

The shoplifter was apprehended in a neighboring store a few weeks later. He spent four nights in jail. The store manager, who sustained a fractured tibial plateau of the knee, spent four months in recovery.

Hardly seems fair—four days versus four months.

Chapter 49
Fishy Shrimp Shoplifting

Shrimp ranks high on the list of shoplifted commodities, especially before Christmas, Thanksgiving, and Easter. We had to adjust our frozen storage areas in the supermarket to accommodate the expected uptick in volume for these prawns.

Fresh shrimp, and previously frozen shrimp, were generally sold from behind the counter, so they were not as apt to be shoplifted as frozen shrimp was, given it was on display in a case and accessible.

One interesting fact about the theft of shrimp is that many of the shoplifters had the added challenge of finding a buyer for their wares before they stole the shellfish.

In a March 5, 2013, article in *The Enterprise*, Maria Papadopoulos reported on the phenomenon.

After the arrest of two Brockton men who allegedly stole nearly one thousand dollars' worth of shrimp from a Norwood supermarket, Papadopoulos reported that Raynham police chief James Donovan said, "Often they already know where they're going to sell it. They don't walk in and steal shrimp and say, 'Gee, where am I going to take this?'"

Brockton Police Lieutenant Paul Bonanca said thieves won't sell to big chain eateries, but instead peddle to bars, small stores, and other independent businesses.

I had a shrimp shoplifter just before Thanksgiving in 2019. The shoplifter walked out of the supermarket with ten, two-pound bags of frozen shrimp, retailing at $19.99 a bag; the incident was reported by a customer.

The shrimp shoplifter had come in with a larger-than-normal shopping bag. He proceeded to get a carriage and nestle the shopping bag in the baby seat of the carriage. The shoplifter headed for the frozen shrimp case at the back of the store. He put ten bags in his carriage then went to a vacant aisle. There, he loaded the shrimp into his shopping bag, left the carriage, and headed to the exit and out the door.

The police were called. There was a very clear picture of our shoplifter exiting the store. He was five-foot-ten, medium build, bald, and had tattoos on both arms. The police were able to identify the shoplifter through social media channels. The shrimp shoplifter lived in the city ten miles from the store. He was a drug user.

The shoplifter pleaded guilty and paid a fine. The supermarket got nothing because, "You can't get blood from a rock," as I had been told before. We were out all that shrimp.

Another shrimp incident happened two weeks before Christmas 2010. A sixty-year-old female shoplifted sixteen two-pound bags of frozen shrimp retailing at $17.69 per bag; total value $300.73. She was seen leaving the supermarket by an alert front-end employee who reported the incident to a manager. The manager managed to catch up to the shoplifter at her car.

She was escorted back into the store and to the office. The police were called. The shoplifter was arrested. It was the busy season at the supermarket with the Christmas holiday, and I never saw what happened to this shoplifter.

On the positive side, we did not lose the shrimp.

Chapter 50
Sandwiches for the Family

Looking back on this incident, I might have handled it differently. I probably should have let the shoplifter go. This happened on the night I usually closed the supermarket. It was a January evening in 2018, around six o'clock. A store employee saw a man walk out of the store with some sandwiches from the prepared food area and reported it to me. I went to the office to see if I could find out what she was talking about.

With a little effort watching video, I saw a tall middle-aged man of medium build take four sandwiches. He proceeded to duck down an aisle close by. He concealed the sandwiches in the pockets of his coat and pants. The total for the sandwiches was less than thirty dollars. At the time, I thought it best to call the police, and I did.

The officer showed up within minutes of my call and came to the office. I showed him pictures of the shoplifter and the police officer said he knew who he was. He asked me if it was alright to go pick this guy up and bring him back to the store to pay for the sandwiches. I didn't have a problem with that; the officer left. I was curious what the relationship was between the shoplifter and the younger officer, but never asked.

About an hour later I was paged to the service center. There was the shoplifter, without the police officer. He asked if we could talk in private, and we proceeded to my office. He apologized for taking the sandwiches. The shoplifter continued to tell me he didn't have any money to pay for them. He explained the sandwiches were to feed his family and took thirty dollars out of his pocket and put the money on my desk.

The shoplifter seemed remorseful. For me, this was probably shoplifter number eight hundred and fifty, and I had heard this type of story before. The sandwich shoplifter also gave me a no trespass notice the officer had filled out; the shoplifter had been told to give it to me.

The shoplifter was from a neighboring town. I wrote up a report and collected the thirty dollars. I took the no trespass notice and never finished filling it out. This shoplifter was not going to be a problem in the future, I determined. I stapled the notice to the shoplifting report.

I explained that there were programs such as the federal supplemental nutrition assistance program, that he could apply to get an EBT card. There were a couple of food pantries in the area that he could go to help feed his family, I also told him.

"This doesn't help me at six o'clock on a Friday night, when my family needs something to eat." Hard to argue with his thought process. I got the feeling he heard this from the police officer as well. The sandwich shoplifter was free to go.

I would bet my paycheck the police officer gave this shoplifter the money to pay for the sandwiches. There are a lot of great police officers out there. It wasn't the first time I had seen one intervene to help.

Epilogue
Thou Shalt Not Steal

Thou shalt not steal. That's one of the ten commandments in the Bible, yet stealing happens every day. It's akin to throwing the tablet through a store's front plate glass window.

I have seen more cases of shoplifting than one might imagine, and I have strong feelings that the punishments should be more stringent. There should be harsher consequences to serve both as punishment and a deterrent.

What can be done to stop the revolving door of steal, pay restitution or fines, and get back in the store to pocket goods? We don't want to go back to the early 1900s and mete out five-year prison sentences for shoplifting. First, there is no room in our prisons, and even I think that punishment is extreme.

So is letting shoplifters off, unpunished.

One idea I have is for our nation's courts to require community restitution, or community service as a mandatory punishment for theft. Having a shoplifter perform community service in the jurisdiction they were caught could be beneficial for towns and cities with strapped municipal budgets. Shoplifters can rake parks, clean streets, spruce up playgrounds, paint municipal buildings. The court system would hold them accountable via a probation officer. A fine could be an alternative, or the fine and service requirements could go hand in hand.

I know that there exists the sentiment that shoplifters steal because they are in need, like the sandwich shoplifter in the last chapter, and while that is sometimes true, we should not focus on what is politically correct but on how to help these people while also deterring crime and removing retail risk. Someone stole something from somebody.

There are resources available—food pantries, food banks, shelters, churches, etc., and are all available for people in need of something to eat. Although not a help in the moment, SNAP—the Supplemental Nutrition Assistance Program, a federal program informally known as "food stamps"—is an option and one could apply for benefits. There are plenty of other choices, besides stealing.

We shouldn't worry about the shoplifters' feelings of embarrassment if they are required to go to court and are then mandated to rake leaves in a public park. I can't worry about that. Shoplifters take risks; they should accept the punishment.

Having said that, I also see that there are many people who need help. Seniors among them. Most seniors I caught did shoplift out of need. Many are existing only on Social Security benefits, which is difficult to say the least. They need to know about food pantries, senior centers, and other resources out there to help.

Many others steal to feed addictions, and those shoplifters should automatically be evaluated by a professional, and they should be granted access to rehabilitation programs; there are hundreds of community rehabilitation programs out there. The addicted stand before a judge. Don't release them back to the street. Match them to a program. We need to connect people to all services.

Shoplifting is the most frequent crime committed in this country today, by both adults and juveniles. Millions of offenses put a drain on retail companies, police officers, and our courts. We need reform, to restore penalties that discourage shoplifting, or the problems will worsen. Shoplifters must once again be held accountable for their actions.

It starts with this simple mandate: Thou shalt not steal.

Acknowledgements

It was my wife, Amy, and daughter, Kelsey, who were instrumental with helping me start this project. It was only with their love, patience, and guidance that I was even able to start writing, using my new laptop. We were in Kiawah Island, South Carolina, for five weeks, and while the girls worked remotely at their respective tasks, I started writing, and with their help, put some chapters together.

A few months later, I printed out three very raw manuscripts and gave them to my good friends Tom Daly, Richard Murphy, and Joe Strem, and I asked for their feedback. Of course, they said all the right things. Thank you for not telling me it was awful; I might have stopped. Thank you, Rich, for connecting me to author Michael Lewis.

Michael, aka Cap'n McNasty, was an open book on all things writing. We had a number of conference calls, and he was so positive and encouraging. Our conversations ran the gauntlet about book writing, editing, publishing. He told me he thought I could get published. Thank you for keeping me going.

I have met or spoken to a number of authors in this last year, at all phases of this project. All had insight, experiences, and advice. I can't thank all of you enough.

Thank you, Noelle Hufnagel, for your advice and saying I could take these chapters to the next level. To Ray Sherman, our weekend editing sessions were very productive and a lot of fun. Thank you, Chris McCarthy, author of three books, for your valuable information on the promotion and sales phase.

I would also like to thank the many colleagues I called to make sure I remembered events as they happened. Thank you to the police officers I contacted to ask about incidents, and thank you for your service. I think I remembered everyone, but if I didn't, thank you for your help and advice.

I would like to thank Destinee Almedia for her wonderful illustrations and book cover art. You are very talented, and I hope this leads into greater projects for you.

Lastly, I would like to thank Janice Beetle. These words are a book because of you. You do what you do, and you do it well, thank you!

About the author

Mark Scamman worked in the supermarket industry for forty-five years. Mark worked for the same company all those years—his only job. The supermarket chain helped him through college, and Mark graduated from the University of Lowell with a bachelor's degree in industrial management. While at the university, he met his wife, Amy. They have two children, Robby and Kelsey, and they live in Dennis Port, Massachusetts.

While working as a manager, Mark managed to get very proficient at catching people who were stealing. Mark learned from the best, and he and his team managed to catch nearly a thousand shoplifters. Mark was named Store Manager of the Year in 1999 by the New Hampshire Grocers Association. One store he managed was named Best Store three years in a row by Best of Central Massachusetts, a survey put on by *The Worcester Telegram and Gazette* yearly.

Mark now enjoys yard work, woodworking, and playing golf with his fellow retirees. He can be reached at markscammanauthor@gmail.com or www.markscamman.com.